# FINDING A JOB IN CANADA

## Other How To Books on Living & Working Abroad

*Other titles in preparation*

The How To series now contains more than 150 titles
in the following categories:

Business Basics
Family Reference
Jobs & Careers
Living & Working Abroad
Student Handbooks
Successful Writing

Please send for a free copy of the latest catalogue for full details
(see back cover for address).

**LIVING & WORKING ABROAD**

# FINDING A JOB IN CANADA

## How to discover well paid work and a great new lifestyle

## Valerie Gerrard

**How To Books**

Cartoons by Mike Flanagan

**British Library Cataloguing in Publication Data**
A catalogue record for this book is available from the British Library.

© Copyright 1996 by Valerie Gerrard.

First published in 1996 by How To Books Ltd, Plymbridge House, Estover
Road, Plymouth PL6 7PZ, United Kingdom. Tel: (01752) 202301.
Fax: (01752) 202331.

Produced for How To Books by Deer Park Productions.
Typeset by PDQ Typesetting, Stoke-on-Trent, Staffs.
Printed and bound by The Cromwell Press, Broughton Gifford, Melksham,
Wiltshire.

# Contents

# List of Illustrations

# Preface

'The best country in the world in which to live.' So said the United Nations, referring to Canada's standard of living. Is it any wonder then that so many people from all over the world fancy making it their home? Over 250,000 people a year emigrate to Canada. And that does not include those who go on working holidays, staying anywhere from five months to several years.

The idea of working in Canada – for either the short, the medium, or the long term – is an attractive prospect for many. Often those who visit Canada on holiday find the way of life very appealing; others respond to the challenge of the 'wide open spaces'. Certainly Canada is large and varied enough to offer an enormous range of opportunities, from the cosmopolitan outlook of cities such as Toronto and Vancouver to the slower yet equally challenging lifestyle of remote areas.

Anyone who is thinking of working in Canada needs to carefully consider many aspects. It's a very big country and there can be a world of difference between city and town, east and west, mountain and prairie. In this book those differences are made clear and you will find out what opportunities are available where. More importantly, you will be led step by step through the whole process of achieving Employment Authorisation, finding the job you want and landing that job.

I have tried to include as much information as possible to help you in your venture. One of the problems with such a vast country is that there is an equally vast amount of contacts. Where these have been too many to list I have indicated where the information can be found. Just about all the references I have given should be easy to find, either when you begin your job search here at home or when you continue it in Canada.

The section on immigration is big, as that is the key to the whole procedure. Without Employment Authorisation you simply will not be able to work in Canada. So wade your way through the information there. Remember that approximately 90 per cent of Skilled Worker applications are successful. I hope you will be, too.

There are addresses throughout the book, as well as in the address section at the back. Often, as in the case of employment consultants and placement agencies, these are just a small sample of the services available. You will come across many more.

In the course of putting this book together I contacted friends and family in Canada, who kindly supplied me with a great deal of information I would probably have had trouble finding this side of the Atlantic. For this help, thanks very much. They did ask me not to paint too rosy a picture of employment prospects in Canada. Unemployment is currently at approximately 8.5 to 9 per cent (varying from province to province) and young Canadians in particular are sometimes finding it difficult to gain full-time employment. Having said that, the opportunities are there if you have the right skills and know where to look.

I hope you enjoy your Canadian adventure and wish you the very best of luck.

*Valerie Gerrard*

# IS THIS YOU?

Aerospace engineer                                          Chef

                 Audiologist

Treatment plant mechanic                    Welding equipment repairer

         Telecommunications specialist

Systems analyst                                          Machinist

                 Millwright

Accountant                                               Administrator

                 Dietician

Mechanical engineer                                    Holiday worker

                 Teacher

Physician                                               IT specialist

                 Nurse

Physiotherapist                                      Electronic engineer

                 Secretary

Machinery repairer                              Farm equipment installer

            Speech pathologist

Cook                                              Occupational therapist

       Construction equipment mechanic

Software programmer                                       Sous-chef

             Nanny/au pair

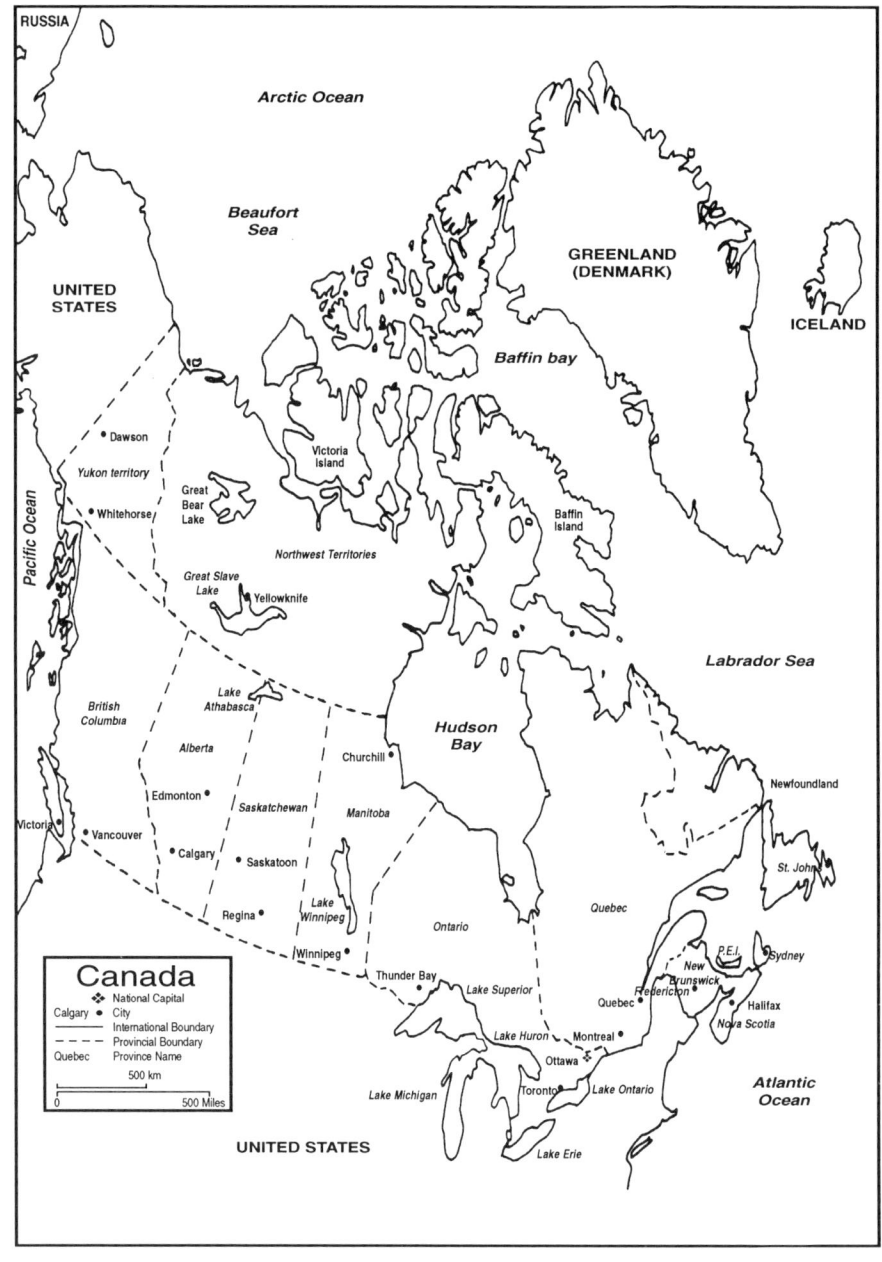

Fig. 1. Map of Canada.

12

# 1
# Deciding to Work in Canada

## LEARNING ABOUT THE COUNTRY

If you are considering working in Canada you probably know something about the country already. This section will help reinforce your knowledge.

### Size and population

Canada covers 9,970,610 square km, which is about the size of all of Europe. Although with the dissolution of the USSR Canada is now the largest country in the world, with 27.3 million inhabitants it ranks twenty-eighth in the world in terms of population. So we really are talking land of the wide open spaces!

It is worth noting, however, that 76.6 per cent of those 27 million live in the major towns and cities, and 31 per cent (8.61 million) are in the three major cities of Toronto, Montreal and Vancouver. (See Figure 2 for details of population distribution by province and territory.)

| CANADIAN POPULATION PERCENTAGE DISTRIBUTION BY PROVINCES AND TERRITORIES (per 1991 census) | | |
|---|---|---|
| Province and Territory | Actual | Percentage |
| Newfoundland | 568,474 | 2.08 |
| Prince Edward Island | 129,765 | 0.46 |
| Nova Scotia | 899, 942 | 3.30 |
| New Brunswick | 723,900 | 2.65 |
| Quebec | 6,895,963 | 25.26 |
| Ontario | 10,084,885 | 36.90 |
| Manitoba | 1,091, 942 | 4.00 |
| Saskatchewan | 988,928 | 3.62 |
| Alberta | 2,545,553 | 9.33 |
| British Columbia | 3,282,061 | 12.02 |
| Yukon | 27,797 | 0.10 |
| Northwest Territories | 57,649 | 0.21 |
| TOTAL | 27,296, 859 | 100.00 |
| Rural | 6,389,724 | |
| Urban | 20,907,135 | |

Fig. 2. Canadian population percentage distribution.

## Climate

It is impossible to give an overall view of the climate of this vast country which stretches from the temperate southern area bordering on the United States to the frozen wastes of the Arctic Circle. Temperatures can range from a summer daytime high of 35°C in some southern areas to daytime winter lows of -25°C in the far north.

## Understanding government structure

If you are coming from Britain you will find the Canadian system of government very familiar. It is based on the British Constitution and is a constitutional monarchy. The Governor General of Canada represents the Queen, the Senate is similar to the UK House of Lords and the main body of government is an elected House of Commons.

What can be confusing for the newcomer is the allocation of power between the **federal** and the **provincial governments**. Canada is comprised of ten **provinces** and two **territories**, each of which has its own autonomous provincial government responsible for education, local taxes, transportation, aspects of health care, *etc.* The federal government, as described above, deals with national issues such as foreign policy, national taxation and the economy.

## UNDERSTANDING THE PEOPLE

### Knowing about multiculturalism

The vast size and varying environments within Canada affect the people and their attitudes. But perhaps the most influential factor is multiculturalism. Canada is officially proud of its multicultural heritage and although not everyone may share this sentiment, most Canadians have, by necessity, a healthy and open attitude towards those from diverse cultures.

This attitude is necessary because of the great number of people from many countries who have made Canada their home over the years. Over 11 million Canadians have some ethnic origin other than British or French, including German, Italian, Ukrainian, Dutch, Polish, Chinese, South Asian, Jewish, Caribbean, Portuguese and Scandinavian.

### Speaking the language

As you are probably aware, there are two official languages in Canada: English and French. Official forms and consumer goods produced in Canada appear with both languages on them. So, if nothing else, English speakers will soon learn the French for 'taxable allowance', 'flakes of corn', and 'free gift inside'.

In fact, 16 per cent of Canadians are bilingual, with 16.1 million having English as their mother tongue and 6.5 million claiming French as their first language. Interestingly, the third most popular language is Chinese.

You will not find it necessary to be bilingual in most parts of Canada, although it would probably be foolish to try to get a job in the Province of Quebec without excellent written and spoken French. No matter where you choose to work, though, you will need to have a good grasp of English and French if you are aiming for any sort of federal government job.

### Not to be confused with...

The United States! If you really want to rile a Canadian, call him an American or say that you can't see much difference between the two countries. There are huge differences: in attitude, culture and politics. And it is true that Canadians are healthier, live longer, spend more on health care and have lower rates of chronic disease than their neighbours to the south.

## FINDING OUT ABOUT THE LIFESTYLE

For three years running the United Nations declared Canada 'the best country in the world in which to live' in terms of lifestyle. Why? Certainly the standard of living, which we will look at more closely, has a lot to do with it, but perhaps it is more the *style* of living that makes Canada so appealing.

### Taking sport seriously

As indicated above, Canada has a great deal of room for manoeuvre and that in itself is a major attraction. It also accounts for the predominantly outdoor nature of the Canadian lifestyle. Sport plays a major part in most people's lives, and it's not just hockey! (Although more than 450,000 Canadian youngsters participate in organised hockey leagues.) All types of team sports such as baseball, soccer, tennis and rugby are popular, as are the more individual recreations like skiing, skating, sailing, windsurfing, *etc.* The varied climate leads to a great diversity in the types of recreation available. There is no doubt that Canadians consider sports of all types an integral part of their lives.

## Recognising the arts

There is a great interest in the arts in Canada. Stratford, Ontario, is home to a Shakespearean company of worldwide repute. Both Vancouver and Montreal have prestigious symphony orchestras. Opera lovers are well served by the Vancouver Opera Association, the Canadian Opera Company and others. Montreal's annual jazz festival is world-renowned. Canada boasts three large ballet companies – the Royal Winnipeg Ballet, Les Grands Ballets Canadiens and the National Ballet of Canada – which perform regularly on the international circuit to great acclaim. Canadian cinema has made quite an impact internationally of late.

Many cities are home to theatre companies, orchestras, opera groups and art galleries of high standard. In the more remote areas such cultural advantages become thinner on the ground but are generally not ignored.

## Attitudes to work

Any observation on a country's attitude to work will be a generalisation, and Canada's vast size and multiculturalism make any such generalisation suspect. However, it would be true to say that the Canadian attitude to work is informal and perhaps less tense than in, say, America or parts of Europe. That is not to say that Canadians do not work hard or have high ambitions, but rather that work is generally seen as only a part (albeit a very important part) of the fabric of life.

## A growing economy

Canada is making an excellent recovery from the worldwide recession. It is estimated that the economy grew by at least 4.6 per cent in 1994 and by 2.3 per cent in 1995. Three per cent growth is estimated for 1996.

Employment figures improved considerably in 1995, with national unemployment at 9.2 per cent at the end of the year. An increasing number of people are working part-time or combining two part-time jobs. The number of part-time jobs in 1994 was virtually double that in 1975 and part-time jobs accounted for almost a quarter of all the jobs in Canada. Moonlighting is very common, particularly amongst 15–24-year olds. Some simply prefer the flexibility of having several part-time jobs, but others have had difficulty finding full-time work. Sadly, the unemployment rate among young people is still high, like most of Europe.

## INVESTIGATING THE STANDARD OF LIVING

Canadians enjoy one of the highest living standards in the world: 83 per cent of families own at least one car, 97.5 per cent have a colour television and one in five owns a personal computer. In 1995 the World Bank named Canadians the second wealthiest people on Earth, pipped to the post only by Australians. This declaration was based on a calculation of the value of natural resources, productive assets and human resources.

### Understanding the economy

Canada is making a rapid recovery from the recent worldwide recession. A member of G7 (the group of seven leading industrialised countries comprised of Canada, France, Germany, Italy, Japan, UK and the USA), Canada showed the second best economic performance of those seven during 1993. Of all the G7 countries only Canada and the United States showed overall employment growth in 1993 (1.2 per cent and 1.5 per cent respectively). As of 1994, inflation was running at less than 2 per cent annually and the unemployment rate is quickly declining.

Figures 10 and 11 in Chapter 3 look at employment statistics in more detail, province by province.

### Reckoning the cost of living

Consumer goods are generally available at prices similar to those in the UK. Where there is a difference Canadian prices tend to be lower. Below is a recent survey of the price per litre of petrol throughout Canada. (Prices are shown in Canadian dollars. Currently the exchange rate is approximately C$2.2 = £1. See the national press for more up to date rates.)

*Price per litre of petrol 1995*

|  | *Regular* | *Premium* |
|---|---|---|
| Average price | 0.53.3 | 0.62.4 |
| Lowest price (Edmonton) | 0.47.3 | 0.56.3 (Toronto and Edmonton) |
| Highest price (Yellowknife) | 0.69.5 | 0.74.2 (Yellowknife) |

```
COST OF LIVING IN CANADA CONSUMER PRICE INDEX 1992
(Base: 1986 = 100)
Food                                               120.8
Housing                                            126.4
Clothing                                           129.5
Transport                                          121.8
Health and personal care                           131.3
Recreation, education and reading                  131.9
Tobacco and alcohol                                169.0
All items                                          128.1
```

Fig. 3. Consumer price index. Source: Statistics Canada, 1992.

## Assessing house prices

The price of housing varies enormously across Canada, with Montreal, Toronto and Vancouver being the most expensive cities in which to buy a home. The least expensive house prices are in Saskatchewan and Manitoba. See Figure 4, which is a specific guide to house prices on a province-by-province basis.

TYPICAL CANADIAN HOUSE PRICES – OCTOBER 1995 (C$000s)

|      | Detached bungalow | 2 Storey house | Condo apt | Townhouse | Senior Exec |
|------|-------------------|----------------|-----------|-----------|-------------|
| BC   | 125-520           | 140-540        | 80-265    | 82-310    | 205-895     |
| Alta | 88-280            | 85-290         | 33-160    | 50-195    | 156-460     |
| Sask | 74-108            | 46-94          | 25-74     | 34-68     | 130-210     |
| Man  | 69-114            | 65-115         | 44-67     | 45-90     | 200         |
| Ont  | 98-300            | 85-286         | 52-185    | 68-240    | 190-840     |
| Que  | 72-160            | 81-280         | 58-154    | 65-140    | 170-875     |
| NB   | 80-104            | 83-135         | 60-65     | 61-95     | 180-226     |
| NS   | 86-129            | 110-172        | 60-127    | 68-118    | 159-262     |
| PEI  | 100               | 120            | 75        | 67        | 210         |
| Nfld | 85-95             | 112-120        | 97        | 65-66     | 180-185     |

Fig. 4. Typical Canadian house prices.

Uncertainty over the future of Quebec province as part of the Canadian nation led to an increase in mortgage rates at the beginning of 1995, but the result of the October referendum on Quebec's sovereignty calmed investors' fears somewhat and at the end of 1995 mortgage rates had fallen again. These rates fluctuate in Canada as elsewhere, but at the time of writing ranged from 7.62 to 8.7 per cent.

- One-year closed mortgage: 7.75 per cent
- Five-year closed mortgage: 8.7 per cent
- Six-month convertible mortgage: 7.62 per cent.

## CONSULTING THE FAMILY

You may find all these facts and figures rather dry, but it really is worth knowing what you are letting yourself in for before you start the sometimes complicated and lengthy process of getting a permit to work in Canada and finding a suitable job. Which leads us to the last part of this chapter: consulting the family. Just a few more facts and figures!

Generally, Canada is a 'family' sort of place. As shown above, recreational facilities are excellent and there is a broad cultural heritage to draw on. Most people have no trouble adapting to what is recognised as a pleasant and easy-going lifestyle.

### Going with your spouse

Realistically, the accompanying partner is most likely to be female so it is worth looking at the role of women in Canada. You will find little difference between the Canadian and the British attitude towards women. The predominant family type is now the dual earner couple, with 60 per cent of women in the labour force. There is still some wage disparity, with women earning on average 72 per cent of what men make for full-time work despite the fact that equal pay for equal work laws have been in place for over a decade.

Women make up 45 per cent of the labour force and 30 per cent of all self-employed persons.

All jurisdictions give the statutory right to maternity leave (usually 17 weeks unpaid). This is in addition to the Federal Unemployment Insurance Scheme which gives 15 weeks of maternity benefits.

### Taking your children

There shouldn't be a great deal of upheaval in terms of education. Canada has had to respond to great cultural diversity and many schools have students from 20 or more distinct ethnocultural groups. For example, in Toronto and Vancouver over half the students in elementary and secondary schools can speak languages other than English or French.

Generally, schooling starts at six (although in some areas kindergarten places are available from four onwards) and is compulsory until 16. Most students, however, stay on until at least 18 years of age. This education is free. Bear in mind that there is no national system – each province is responsible for its own arrangements. For further details contact:

> The Canadian School Boards Association
> #505, 124 O'Connor Street
> Ottawa, ON K1P 5M8.

*The School Solution* is a guide to Canada's schools which includes information on pre-school programmes, elementary and secondary education, out of school activities and curriculum details. It is obtainable from:

> Canada Information Services
> Suite 421, 253 College St
> Toronto, ON M5T 1R5.

This is, by the way, a good source for other information about Canada. They will send a list of other publications available with your order form.

Many independent schools are also available. For more information contact:

> The Conference of Independent Schools
> PO Box 182
> Port Hope, ON L1A 3W3.

University and post-secondary education is widely available and, again, varies from province to province. Once you have an idea of what area of Canada you will relocate to you can write for guidance to:

> The Canadian Society for the Study of Higher Education
> #1001, 151 Slater Street
> Ottawa, ON K1P 5N1.

You can also obtain a comprehensive guide to Canadian universities entitled *U-Choose – A Guide to Canadian Universities* from:

> Moving Publications Ltd
> 4 Upjohn St, Ste 100
> Don Mills, ON M3B 2W1
> Tel: (416) 441 1168. Fax: (416) 441 1641.

This guide lists approximately 60 universities, and outlines admission requirements, courses/programmes offered, fees, housing/ residence, library resources, athletic programmes and facilities *etc.* Other organisations which can provide information on Canadian education include:

Youth and Student Information
Association of Student Councils
171 College St
Toronto, ON M5T 1PZ.

Canadian Bureau for International Education
85 Albert St, 14th Flr
Ottawa, ON K1P 6A4.

**Agreeing your plans**
Finally, it cannot be stressed enough that all members of your family who are going to accompany you must be considered. They are going to have to live there too, and while you may be looking forward to spending your leisure time shushing down the slopes with your ski-mad son your wife may be allergic to snow and your daughter may have a fear of heights! Be sure to talk it over with everyone concerned and make sure they have as many facts as possible. The various provincial tourist boards can send you very useful information that will give everybody a good idea of what they are heading for. See the address section at the end of this book for a list of tourist board offices.

**CHECKLIST**

• Canada is committed to multiculturalism. Over 11 million Canadians have some ethnic origin other than British or French.

• Federal government is run along very similar lines to that in Britain. Be aware of the importance of the provincial governments, which control education, local taxes and other areas.

• The United Nations declared Canada 'the best country in the world in which to live'.

• There is a strong emphasis on outdoor activities and sport.

• The Canadian attitude to work may be more 'laid back' than you are used to.

- The national economy is recovering well from the world-wide recession, with 3 per cent growth estimated for 1996. Unemployment was 9.2 per cent at the end of 1995 and expected to continue to fall in 1996.

- Educational facilities are good and similar to those in Britain. They do, however, vary from province to province.

- Canada is *not* to be confused with the United States! Canadians do not appreciate what they consider to be an unflattering comparison.

## CASE STUDIES

Let's take a look at three people who are thinking about moving to and working in Canada. Each has different expectations and priorities. We will consider their individual needs, the problems they might encounter and how these difficulties can be resolved.

### Samantha Curry seeks a complete change

Samantha is looking for a complete change of lifestyle. She is bored with her life in Britain and her job as a dietitian at the local hospital. She visited Vancouver on holiday last year and fell in love with the lifestyle there. She is 24 years old and single, living at home with her widowed mother. Sam doesn't intend to move to Canada for the rest of her life, but would like to try it for a few years.

Having already visited Canada, Samantha has a fairly good, if perhaps superficial, idea of the lifestyle there. She is determined that she wants to live and work in Canada for a few years but her widowed mother, whose impression of Canada is one of Eskimos and frozen wastes, is concerned.

Samantha shows her mother some of the information she has already gathered about Canada, pointing out that almost 80 per cent of Canadians live in major towns and cities.

'For three years in a row the United Nations named Canada the best place in the world to live. They can't have been talking about living in igloos, can they?' Sam points out.

Sam's mother is a bit more comfortable with the idea, but still feels she needs to know a lot more before she will be happy about it.

### George Robins wants to further his career

A 38-year old electronics engineer, George has felt for some time that his career has not been progressing as he would wish. He wants to work in a more forward-looking country, but does not fancy moving himself, his wife and two young children to the United States. He sees Canada as the ideal compromise. Although nervous about the move, his family support his ambition and are willing to take up a new life in Canada.

George gathers the family together for a discussion. His wife is concerned about how they will fit in.

'Won't they think of us as foreign?' she wonders. 'And we don't speak French.'

George explains the multicultural aspect of Canadian life. His wife is surprised to learn that people of so many nationalities make their home there.

'And French is only one of the official languages,' George points out. 'In most parts you don't need it at all.'

George and his family realise that they have quite a bit still to learn about life in Canada and decide to get some books from the library. After studying these they become quite excited at the prospect.

### Lucy Martin thinks the grass may be greener

Lucy has not worked since leaving school with two A-Levels three years ago. She has always toyed with the idea of emigrating to Canada, as her late mother was Canadian and always spoke longingly of her early life there. She has no close family ties in England, but has an aunt and uncle whom she has never met living in Montreal. They are willing to help her out when she arrives.

Lucy is not too bothered about what sort of work she does, although she has a romantic ideal of a rugged, outdoor life far from the pressures of the modern world.

A friend points out, 'You'll still have to work for a living, you know. I can't see you landing a job as a lumberjack.'

Lucy replies, 'I'm sure there must be lots of things I can do once I get there.'

'Perhaps you should find out a bit more about the place before you start making plans,' her friend suggests.

'I'm sure there will be no problem,' Lucy insists, thus letting herself in for some unpleasant surprises.

### DISCUSSION POINTS

1. How do you think your way of life will change when you move to Canada? There are many positive points; can you think of anything which might be a negative factor?

2. How will the multicultural elements of Canadian life affect you? Your family? Would you regard this as a negative or positive feature?

3. Some people who move from Britain to Canada react badly to the vastness of the country and the greatly increased space. Might this prove a problem for you?

4. Do you know anyone who has emigrated to Canada? Could you get in touch with them and find out about their experience? Could they give you any tips?

# 2
# Dealing with Immigration

## UNDERSTANDING THE PROCESS

Many factors are involved in your search for a job in Canada: location, duration, the job itself. One thing, however, is essential in all cases. You will have to obtain permission to work in Canada from the Canadian High Commission. For that reason this chapter is a fairly long and detailed one, to give you a complete understanding of the immigration process and how to successfully make your way through it.

Generally, you stand a chance of getting an immigrant visa if:

- You have a good education.

- Your employment skills are applicable to the Canadian labour market.

- You have the necessary language and communications skills (English and/or French).

- You are of good character.

- You are in good health.

## Three visa routes
There are three basic routes via which immigrants are admitted to Canada:

1. **Family class.** A sponsored immigration programme designed to reunite families.

2. **Refugee and Humanitarian Class.**

3. **Independent Class.** This is the one we will look at in detail. It includes skilled workers, entrepreneurs, investors and self-employed persons.

Within the Independent Class there are three different types of applicant to consider.

1. A skilled worker requesting permanent status.

2. A temporary, vacation or exchange worker.

3. An entrepreneur or business person intending to start a business in Canada.

The vast majority will gain their permits via the first route.

## Starting the process

Although the process can appear complicated it is in fact fairly simple, being based on a points system. Further on in this chapter we will look at how cases are assessed and you will be able to work out for yourself what your points total is likely to be.

In many cases the application will be straightforward and with the help of this book and the information you will receive from the Canadian High Commission you will be able to complete the process without any other assistance. Once you have filled in all the forms and provided all the information required, the Canadian High Commission will let you know how things stand within twelve weeks. If all is well, your visa will be issued at that time. If there are queries or problems they will advise that an interview or additional processing is necessary. If you do not meet their requirements they will give a written explanation.

## Spotting likely difficulties

The areas that can cause difficulties include criminal convictions, lack of training and health problems. There are agencies and firms which will help you overcome those obstacles, and these are dealt with in detail later in this chapter.

There is one more wrinkle. If you are intending to immigrate to Quebec the process is slightly different. That, too, will be outlined in this chapter.

## Being aware of changes to requirements

Please note that the information on the immigration procedure and requirements is correct at the time of writing. However, the Canadian government has announced its intention to slightly modify the selection criteria some time in 1996. That won't change the actual process, but will have an effect on how points are awarded. The major change is expected to be a greater emphasis on English and French language ability, and education. You will receive full, up-to-date details by writing to:

The Immigration and Medical Division of the Canadian High
Commission
38 Grosvenor St
London W1X 0AA.

## MEETING THE REQUIREMENTS

### Applying as a skilled worker requesting permanent status

The majority of applicants will fall into this category. This category
applies to you if you are not:

* aiming for a temporary permit or
* intending to start a business in Canada.

The first and most important step is to look at the Detailed General
Occupations List at the end of this book. If your occupation is not
shown there you should probably leap straight to the last section of this
chapter and consider engaging the services of an immigration
consultant or attorney. Do bear in mind, however, that you may
qualify under another heading. For example, a plumber might qualify
as a pipe fitter.

Your professional qualifications may not be acceptable as such in the
Canadian labour market. The best way to find out is to visit a reference
library and consult the *Canadian Almanac & Directory*. There you will
find relevant professional organisations in Canada which will be able
to advise you whether your qualifications are suitable. Alternatively
you could contact:

The Canadian Information Centre for International Credentials
252 Bloor West, Suite 5-200
Toronto, ON M5S IV5.
Tel: (416) 964 2551. Fax: (416) 964 2296.

### Key criteria for skilled worker applicants

Once you have established the points value of your occupation you can
continue to assess your chances on the following criteria:

* Age.

* Education.

* Specific vocational preparation (SVP). This is the level of training
  needed to work in your occupation in Canada.

- Occupation.

- Pre-arranged employment (note that this applies only when a Canada Employment Centre has certified that there is no suitably qualified and available Canadian or permanent resident to fill the position).

- Designated occupation (extra points are awarded for special occupations in particular provinces; these are marked with an * on the Occupations List).

- Work experience.

- Language ability.

- Demographic factor (you won't be able to assess this yourself as it is a figure set by the Canadian government).

- Personal suitability.

- Relatives in Canada.

A fairly long list, but not really complicated if you go through it one by one.

*Age (maximum 10 points)*

| Age | Points |
|---|---|
| 18 | 4 |
| 19 | 6 |
| 20 | 8 |
| 21–44 | 10 |
| 45 | 8 |
| 46 | 6 |
| 47 | 4 |
| 48 | 2 |
| 49 + | 0 |

*Education (maximum 16 points)*

| | Points |
|---|---|
| • Not completed secondary school. | 0 |
| • Completed secondary school but not eligible for university and do not have a trade or occupational certification. | 5 |
| • Completed secondary school and eligible for university. | 10 |

- Completed secondary school with a trade or occupational certification.                                                    10

- Completed a post-secondary programme such as college, trade school diploma or apprenticeship which did not require university entrance level schooling. Must have included at least one year of full-time classroom study.     10

- Completed a post-secondary programme as above, but which required secondary schooling to university entrance level.     13

- Completed a university degree requiring at least three years of full-time study.                                          15

- Completed a second- or third-level university degree, *eg* Masters, PhD.                                                  16

*Specific vocational preparation (maximum 18 points)*
This refers to the length of training, education and/or apprenticeship that is required to work at your occupation in Canada. Refer to the Detailed General Occupations List. Award yourself the number of points listed under the column SVP for your occupation.

If your occupation is not on the list but you have arranged employment which has been validated by a Canada Employment Centre, you will have been notified of the relevant SVP points. Add these here.

*Occupation (maximum 10 points)*
Again, refer to the Detailed General Occupations List. You must score at least one point in the occupation factor to be accepted unless:

1. You have a designated occupation with a SVP of 11 or more (per the Occupations List), in which case score 10.

or

2. You have arranged employment that has been validated by a Canadian Employment Centre.

*Pre-arranged employment/designated occupation factor (10 points)*
*Points*
- You have arranged employment or have a designated occupation (per the Occupations List).                                 10

● You are a member of the clergy and have a letter offering a permanent salaried position from a congregation in Canada.          10

● Your family in Canada has a business in which you will work full-time. Note that this process must be initiated in Canada; your relative should contact the nearest Canada Immigration Centre and ask about the Family Business Scheme.          10

*Work experience (maximum 8 points)*
This must be worked out on the basis of the number of years experience you have in your intended occupation after completion of formal training, and the number of points allocated for SVP (see Detailed General Occupations List). Use the following table to calculate the points for work experience. Note that if you do not score points in this category your application will be refused, so you must have at least one year's experience in your occupation to proceed.

| SVP Points | 1 yr | 2 yrs | 3 yrs | 4 yrs + |
|---|---|---|---|---|
| 1–3 | score 2 | score 2 | score 2 | score 2 |
| 5–7 | score 2 | score 4 | score 4 | score 4 |
| 11–15 | score 2 | score 4 | score 6 | score 6 |
| 18 | score 2 | score 4 | score 6 | score 8 |

*Language ability (maximum 15 points)*
If you are fluent in both English and French, score 15 points. If not, use the following table to calculate your points. Note that either English or French can be your first language, but no other languages are taken into consideration in this calculation.

| 1st language | Read | Write | Speak |
|---|---|---|---|
| Fluent | 3 | 3 | 3 |
| Well | 2 | 2 | 2 |
| With difficulty | 0 | 0 | 0 |
| 2nd language | | | |
| Fluent | 2 | 2 | 2 |
| Well | 1 | 1 | 1 |
| With difficulty | 0 | 0 | 0 |

For example, if English is your first language and you are fluent in all aspects of it you will score 9 points. If you are also able to speak French reasonably well, but can only read and write a few basic words, you will score an additional 2 points, making a total of 11.

*Demographic factor*
This is an unknown element, as it is awarded by the Canadian government. As a general rule, give yourself 8 points in this section.

*Personal suitability (maximum 10 points)*
This is also an unknown, as it is assessed by a visa officer who considers your adaptability, motivation, initiative and resourcefulness. The average applicant is given 5–7 points so, for the purpose of self-assessment award yourself 6 points here.

*Relative in Canada (bonus 5 points)*
Do you have a brother, sister, mother, father, grandparent, aunt, uncle, niece or nephew living in Canada? If they are a permanent resident or Canadian citizen, score an extra 5 points.

*Assessing your score*
What you are aiming for is a score of at least 70 points. If that is not achieved, the application is refused. There really is no point in applying if you do not come into that range. Bear in mind that the figure you have come up with is still only a guess, largely because of the demographic factor which is set by the Canadian government and the personal suitability factor, which is assessed by a visa officer at the time of your application.

*Applying as a temporary, exchange or vacation worker*
You will be granted a temporary work visa if your skills are in high demand and you can provide economic benefits to Canada. In most cases you will need to have a job offer from a Canadian employer before the visa is granted.
   This applies even to young people looking for vacation employment. Your best bet in this case is to contact BUNAC's Work Canada Programme which is designed for young people who do not have a job offer or who are interested in working temporarily in Canada on a more flexible basis. See address section for contact details.

*Obtaining Employment Authorisation*
If you have a Canadian job offer (which, as in the case of a permanent resident application, must be certified by a Canadian Employment Centre) you should apply to the Canadian High Commission for **Employment Authorisation** (a work permit). This is usually valid for five months and is not transferable between jobs.
   You may be able to obtain Employment Authorisation that allows

for swapping jobs, but it is not the norm. In some cases your authorisation may be valid for up to three years.

The key to temporary authorisation is proof that there are no Canadian citizens or landed immigrants available to carry out the job.

Teachers *etc* on exchange visits must also obtain Employment Authorisation, but this will normally be handled by the association or agency arranging the exchange.

## Applying as an entrepreneur or business person intending to start a business in Canada

If you fall within this category your application will be given priority treatment and your chances of success are very good. Known as the **Business Immigration Scheme**, this is a fairly recent category aimed at entrepreneurs, investors and the self-employed. You should contact the Immigration and Medical Division of the Canadian High Commission for complete details, but the following will give you a brief outline of how the scheme works.

*Entrepreneur category*
This applies to someone who is experienced in business, and who intends to buy or establish a business which will create jobs for one or more Canadians and make a significant contribution to the economy. Successful applicants are granted a conditional visa. Within two years of the visa being issued they must establish a business which employs at least one Canadian. You will need to prove that you have sufficient funds to accomplish this.

*Investor category*
To qualify for the investor category you must have successfully operated, controlled or directed a business or commercial undertaking and have accumulated a net worth of minimum C$500,000. You will then be required to make a minimum investment in Canadian business (from C$250,000 to C$500,000 depending on province and certain other conditions). Once this is done you apply for an immigrant visa, which will be issued if you and all your dependants meet all other Canadian immigration requirements (good health and character, *etc.*).

*Self-employed category*
Finally within the Business Immigration Scheme is the self-employed person category. This describes someone who intends to purchase or set up a small business in Canada that will create employment for himself and make a significant contribution to the economy, cultural or artistic

life of that country. No minimum investment level exists, but the applicant must be able to satisfy immigration officials that he has sufficient funds to set up a business and maintain himself and his dependants.

## Immigration to Quebec

The procedure is much the same but the points awarded for occupation are geared to the opportunities for employment in Quebec. You should obtain your form from the Quebec Immigration Service. The nearest office to the UK is:

Service d'Immigration du Québec
Délégation générale du Québec
46 avenue des Arts, 7 étage
1040 Bruxelles, Belgium.
Tel: (322) 512 0036. Fax: (322) 514 2641.

You will be sent a preliminary questionnaire. If the information you provide on that form is satisfactory you will then receive a second, more detailed questionnaire. If that is approved you will be called to attend an interview with an immigration adviser. A successful interview will result in receipt of a **Quebec Selection Certificate** a few weeks later.

Up to this point you will not be required to pay any fees (except in the case of a Business applicant). Once you have your Quebec Selection Certificate you join up again with the general Canadian immigration system and will need to complete medical and legal assessments. Fees are chargeable for this process. The whole thing takes from six to twelve months.

## Universal requirements

There are two factors that apply no matter what category you apply under. If you have a problem with either of these there is not much point in lodging your application without seeking assistance from an immigration consultant or attorney.

*Proving your 'good character'*

All immigrants must be of 'good character'. This means that if you have a criminal record you are not going to get a visa. And it is up to you to prove your good record. You will have to provide a police certificate/clearance from each country in which you have lived for six months or more in the last ten years. This also applies to all your dependants aged 18 or over.

If you or any of your dependants do have a criminal conviction in the past it is almost certain that your application will be refused. There is one small glimmer of hope, however. In exceptional circumstances those with criminal convictions may be admitted to Canada on the grounds that they have been 'rehabilitated'. You may not apply for approval for rehabilitation until five years after the end of your sentence.

*Passing a medical*
The other universal criterion is health. You will not be granted a visa if you 'present a health risk or danger to Canadians' or are 'likely to place an excessive demand on Canada's health or social services'. You and all your dependants, whether they are accompanying you to Canada or not, must pass a medical in accordance with the above. This examination must be performed by a physician designated by the Canadian Immigration and Medical Division. You will be given a list of approved doctors along with your application forms.

## APPLYING FOR A VISA

Having established that you are in with a chance, you now need to start the actual process. Remember, though, there is no point in even making the application if it does not look like you will tot up 70 points per the allocations outlined above. That is not to say that you should give up on the whole thing, simply that you will have to do whatever is necessary to increase your points (another year's experience in your job, perhaps, or some additional education). If you think your application is borderline you may decide to get assistance from an immigration consultant or attorney.

Assuming that you are going ahead on your own, here is your step-by-step guide to getting a visa. The following applies if you fall into the first category of skilled worker requesting permanent status. Granting of a temporary visa is usually dependent on a job offer in Canada, and the Business Immigrant Scheme follows a different set of guidelines which are outlined above.

### Getting the ball rolling
First write, telephone or visit the **Immigration Division** of the Canadian High Commission in London. They will send you a full set of application forms, including medical and legal forms.

### Completing the forms
You will receive:

- Immigration Application Form
- request for Police Certificates/Clearances
- a comprehensive guide to completing the forms
- list of physicians approved to carry out the medical.

Now you can start the mammoth task of completing the forms for everybody in your family who is over 18 years of age at the time of the application, regardless of whether they will accompany you to Canada.

*The Application Form*
Figure 5 shows the Application Form which will give your visa officer the basic information he needs to assess your points. Note that you will need to include photocopies of all your educational, trade and professional qualifications along with evidence of your employment experience. Personal documents such as passports and birth certificates are also required.

*The Request for Police Certificates/Clearance*
This is your responsibility. Figure 6 is a sample of the form that you must send to the relevant authorities in any countries in which you have lived in the last ten years.

*The Medical Report Form*
The form shown in Figure 7 must be completed by a doctor authorised by Canada Immigration.

*Submitting the forms*
Having done all that, and followed the accompanying instructions to the letter, you will give all your documents and the fee to the examining doctor. He will forward this to the Immigration Department who will then decide if an interview is necessary.

*The Immigration Visa Processing Fee*
At the time of writing the fee schedule is:

|  | *Immigrant Visa Processing Fee* | *Right of Landing Fee* |
|---|---|---|
| Principal applicant | C$500 | C$975 |
| Spouse | C$500 | C$975 |
| Each dependant 19 years and over | C$500 | C$975 |
| Each dependant under 19 years | C$100 | n/a |

# M95-2000

PROTECTED WHEN COMPLETED

**▮✦▮** Employment and Immigration Canada    Emploi et Immigration Canada

| • FOR OFFICE USE ONLY • |
|---|
| OFFICE FILE NUMBER (OR IMM 134) CASE LABEL) |

## IMMIGRANT APPLICATION FORM
### (APPLICATION FOR PERMANENT RESIDENCE IN CANADA)

I AM APPLYING AS A: PRINCIPAL APPLICANT ☐    DEPENDENT ☐

| 1 | MY SURNAME (FAMILY NAME) IS: | MY FIRST NAME IS: | MY OTHER NAMES ARE: |
|---|---|---|---|

MY FULL NAME IN THE SCRIPT OF MY NATIVE LANGUAGE IS (E.G. ARABIC SCRIPT, CYRILLIC ALPHABET, CHINESE, KOREAN OR JAPANESE CHARACTERS):

| 2 | ALL OTHER NAMES I HAVE USED ARE: (INCLUDE MAIDEN NAME IF APPLICABLE) | 3 | SEX   MALE ☐   FEMALE ☐ |
|---|---|---|---|

| 4 | MY DATE AND PLACE OF BIRTH ARE:   DAY MONTH YEAR | CITY OR TOWN | COUNTRY | 5 | I AM A CITIZEN OF |
|---|---|---|---|---|---|

| 6 | MY PERMANENT HOME ADDRESS IS: | 7 | MY CURRENT MAILING ADDRESS IS: |
|---|---|---|---|
| | | | ☐ SAME AS IN QUESTION **6** OR: |
| | MY TELEPHONE NUMBER IS: ▶ | | |

| 8 | MY PRESENT MARITAL STATUS IS: (CHECK MORE THAN ONE AS APPLICABLE) |
|---|---|
| | NEVER MARRIED ☐   ENGAGED ☐   MARRIED ☐   WIDOWED ☐   SEPARATED ☐   DIVORCED ☐   MY TELEPHONE NUMBER IS: ▶ |

| 9 | DATE AND PLACE OF MY MARRIAGE   DAY MONTH YEAR | CITY OR TOWN | COUNTRY | 10 | I HAVE BEEN MARRIED MORE THAN ONCE   YES ☐   NO ☐   IF "YES" STATE NUMBER OF TIMES ▶ |
|---|---|---|---|---|---|

**11**   PERSONAL DETAILS OF ALL MY DEPENDENTS (start with spouse in Item A)

| | FAMILY NAME | FIRST NAME | OTHER NAMES | DATE OF BIRTH DAY MONTH YEAR | MARITAL STATUS (PLEASE SPECIFY AS IN 8 ABOVE) | RELATIONSHIP TO ME | TO ACCOMPANY ME TO CANADA |
|---|---|---|---|---|---|---|---|
| A | | | | | | SPOUSE | YES ☐ NO ☐ |
| B | | | | | | | YES ☐ NO ☐ |
| C | | | | | | | YES ☐ NO ☐ |
| D | | | | | | | YES ☐ NO ☐ |
| E | | | | | | | YES ☐ NO ☐ |
| F | | | | | | | YES ☐ NO ☐ |
| G | | | | | | | YES ☐ NO ☐ |
| H | | | | | | | YES ☐ NO ☐ |
| I | | | | | | | YES ☐ NO ☐ |

**12**   PASSPORT DETAILS FOR PRINCIPAL APPLICANT AND FOR PERSONS LISTED IN QUESTION 11 (to be completed by principal applicant only)

| | FIRST NAME | PASSPORT NUMBER | PLACE OF BIRTH (MUST BE COMPLETED) | CITIZEN OF | DATE OF EXPIRY DAY MO YEAR | IDENTITY CARD NO |
|---|---|---|---|---|---|---|
| | PRINCIPAL APPLICANT | | | | | |
| A | SPOUSE | | | | | |
| B | | | | | | |
| C | | | | | | |
| D | | | | | | |
| E | | | | | | |
| F | | | | | | |
| G | | | | | | |
| H | | | | | | |
| I | | | | | | |

IMM 0008 (11-95) LONDON E     **THIS FORM HAS BEEN ESTABLISHED BY THE MINISTER OF EMPLOYMENT AND IMMIGRATION**

Canada

Fig. 5. Immigration application form.

| **3** | ABILITY IN ENGLISH | ABILITY IN FRENCH |
|---|---|---|
| SPEAK | FLUENTLY ☐   WELL ☐   WITH DIFFICULTY ☐   NOT AT ALL ☐ | FLUENTLY ☐   WELL ☐   WITH DIFFICULTY ☐   NOT AT ALL ☐ |
| READ ▶ | FLUENTLY ☐   WELL ☐   WITH DIFFICULTY ☐   NOT AT ALL ☐ | FLUENTLY ☐   WELL ☐   WITH DIFFICULTY ☐   NOT AT ALL ☐ |
| WRITE | FLUENTLY ☐   WELL ☐   WITH DIFFICULTY ☐   NOT AT ALL ☐ | FLUENTLY ☐   WELL ☐   WITH DIFFICULTY ☐   NOT AT ALL ☐ |

» MY MOTHER TONGUE IS

**4** MY EDUCATION (INDICATE NUMBER OF YEARS OF SCHOOL SUCCESSFULLY COMPLETED)

| YEARS OF ELEMENTARY/ PRIMARY SCHOOL | YEARS OF SECONDARY/ HIGH SCHOOL | YEARS OF UNIVERSITY/ COLLEGE | YEARS OF FORMAL APPRENTICESHIP/TRAINING |
|---|---|---|---|
| | | | |

**5** DETAILS OF MY POST SECONDARY EDUCATION

| DATES FROM M Y | TO M Y | NAME OF INSTITUTION (INCLUDING APPRENTICESHIP TRAINING) | CITY AND COUNTRY | TYPE OF CERTIFICATE OR DIPLOMA ISSUED |
|---|---|---|---|---|
| | | | | |
| | | | | |
| | | | | |
| | | | | |

**6** MY PRESENT OCCUPATION IS | CURRENT GROSS MONTHLY EARNINGS | **17** MY INTENDED OCCUPATION IN CANADA IS

**8** MY WORK HISTORY FOR THE PAST 10 YEARS (PROVIDE DETAILS ON A SEPARATE SHEET AS REQUIRED)

| DATES FROM M Y | TO M Y | NAME OF EMPLOYER (WRITE NAME IN FULL. DO NOT USE ABBREVIATIONS) | CITY AND COUNTRY | MY OCCUPATION |
|---|---|---|---|---|
| | | | | |
| | | | | |
| | | | | |
| | | | | |
| | | | | |

**9** THE FOLLOWING PERSON, EMPLOYER OR ORGANIZATION IN CANADA HAS OFFERED TO ASSIST ME AFTER ARRIVAL (NAME AND ADDRESS AND COPY OF JOB OFFER, IF YOU HAVE ONE) | **20** RELATIONSHIP TO ME OF PERSON NAMED IN 19

**21** DESTINATION IN CANADA

| NAME OF CITY/TOWN | PROVINCE |
|---|---|
| | |

**2** I HAVE THE FOLLOWING ASSETS: (SHOW AMOUNT OR VALUE)

| TRANSFERABLE MONEY | PROPERTY | MONTHLY TRANSFERABLE PENSION | OTHER |
|---|---|---|---|
| | | | |

IF "OTHER", GIVE DETAILS HERE ▶

**3** I HAVE THE FOLLOWING DEBTS OR LEGAL OBLIGATIONS (e g CHILD SUPPORT PAYMENTS) OWING TO: (GIVE NAME OF PERSON(S) OR ORGANIZATION)

| | TOTAL DEBT's (AMOUNT) |
|---|---|
| | |
| | |
| | |
| | |

**24** DURING THE PAST 10 YEARS I HAVE LIVED AT THE FOLLOWING ADDRESSES

| DATES | | | | STREET AND NUMBER | CITY OR TOWN | COUNTRY |
|---|---|---|---|---|---|---|
| FROM | | TO | | | | |
| M | Y | M | Y | | | |
| | | | | | | |
| | | | | | | |
| | | | | | | |
| | | | | | | |

**25** SINCE MY 18th BIRTHDAY, I HAVE BEEN (OR STILL AM) A MEMBER OF, OR ASSOCIATED WITH THE FOLLOWING POLITICAL, SOCIAL, YOUTH, STUDENT OR VOCATIONAL ORGANIZATIONS (INCLUDING TRADE UNIONS AND PROFESSIONAL ASSOCIATIONS). INCLUDE ANY MILITARY SERVICE (SHOW RANK, UNIT AND LOCATION OF SERVICE IN LAST COLUMN)

| DATES | | | | NAME AND ADDRESS OF ORGANIZATION | TYPE OF ORGANIZATION | POSITION HELD (IF ANY) |
|---|---|---|---|---|---|---|
| FROM | | TO | | | | |
| M | Y | M | Y | | | |
| | | | | | | |
| | | | | | | |
| | | | | | | |

**26**

| MY PARENTS | DATE OF BIRTH D M Y | CITY, TOWN AND COUNTRY OF BIRTH | PRESENT ADDRESS IN FULL (IF DECEASED GIVE DATE) |
|---|---|---|---|
| FATHER'S FULL NAME | | | |
| MOTHER'S FULL NAME BEFORE MARRIAGE | | | |

**27** HAVE YOU OR HAS ANY ONE OF THE PERSONS IN QUESTION 11 EVER (ANSWER "YES" OR "NO")

**A** HAD ANY SERIOUS DISEASE OR PHYSICAL OR MENTAL DISORDER? _____

**B** BEEN CONVICTED OF OR CURRENTLY CHARGED WITH ANY CRIME OR OFFENCE IN ANY COUNTRY? _____

**C** APPLIED PREVIOUSLY FOR AN IMMIGRANT OR VISITOR VISA TO CANADA? _____

**D** BEEN REFUSED AN IMMIGRANT OR VISITOR VISA TO CANADA OR ANY OTHER COUNTRY? _____

**E** BEEN REFUSED ADMISSION TO, OR ORDERED TO LEAVE CANADA OR ANY OTHER COUNTRY? _____

**F** IN PERIODS OF EITHER PEACE OR WAR, HAVE YOU EVER BEEN INVOLVED IN THE COMMISSION OF A WAR CRIME OR CRIME AGAINST HUMANITY, SUCH AS WILLFUL KILLING, TORTURE, ATTACKS UPON, ENSLAVEMENT, STARVATION OR OTHER INHUMANE ACTS COMMITTED AGAINST CIVILIANS OR PRISONERS OF WAR, OR DEPORTATION OF CIVILIANS? _____

IF THE ANSWER TO ANY OF THE ABOVE IS "YES" PROVIDE DETAILS HERE _____

**28** **PRINCIPAL APPLICANT:** ATTACH TWO PASSPORT SIZE PHOTOGRAPHS OF YOURSELF AND EACH PERSON UNDER AGE 18 LISTED IN ITEM 11

**SPOUSE OR DEPENDENT CHILDREN** AGE 18 OR OVER. ATTACH TWO PHOTOGRAPHS OF YOURSELF ON YOUR SEPARATE APPLICATION FORM. ALL PHOTOGRAPHS SHOULD BE IDENTIFIED BY WRITING THE SUBJECT'S NAME AND DATE OF BIRTH ON THE REVERSE ON THE PHOTOGRAPH.

**29** AUTHORITY TO DISCLOSE PERSONAL INFORMATION

A. I hereby authorize all governmental authorities, including all police, judicial and state authorities in all the countries in which I have resided, to release to the Canadian Government authorities all records and information that they may possess on my behalf concerning any investigations, arrests, charges, trials, convictions and sentences. I understand that this information will be used to assist in evaluating my suitability for admission to Canada, or any other reason, pursuant to Canadian Immigration Legislation.

B. I understand that, having applied for permanent residence in Canada, I (and my dependants) may be required to undergo a medical examination, and I therefore consent to the release of specific details concerning the medical condition of myself (and my dependants if applicable), as may be relevant to my admission to Canada, to the following: Immigration and Visa Officers; authorities of Health & Welfare Canada and the province of my destination; my sponsor in Canada; the Immigration Appeal Division and other judicial bodies.

C. I further authorize Canadian government authorities to release, as necessary, any personal financial information or corporate financial information of which I am the proprietor to the appropriate government authorities of the province of my destination. I understand that this information will be used to assist in evaluating my suitability for admission to Canada, or any other reason, pursuant to Canadian Immigration Legislation.

D. I also authorize the release of information from my Immigration records to: (check one or more)

☐ The individual named hereinafter: _____
(Name of individual)

☐ My sponsor

☐ My Canadian representative (if any)

Name of Individual _____ Name of Firm _____

Signature of applicant: _____ Date: _____

**30** DECLARATION OF APPLICANT

• I declare that the information I have given in this application is truthful, complete and correct.

• I understand that any false statements or concealment of a material fact may result in my exclusion from Canada, and even though I should be admitted to Canada for permanent residence a fraudulent entry on this application may be grounds for my prosecution and/or removal.

• Should my answers to questions 8, 11 or 27, change at any time prior to my departure for Canada, I undertake to report such change and delay my departure until I have been informed in writing, by the office dealing with my application, that I may proceed to Canada.

• I understand all the foregoing statements, having asked for and obtained an explanation on every point which was not clear to me.

Signature of applicant: _____ Date: _____

**DO NOT COMPLETE THE FOLLOWING SECTION NOW.** YOU MAY BE ASKED TO SIGN IT IN THE PRESENCE OF A REPRESENTATIVE OF THE CANADIAN GOVERNMENT OR OFFICIAL APPOINTED BY THE CANADIAN GOVERNMENT.

**31** SOLEMN DECLARATION

I,_____ SOLEMNLY DECLARE THAT THE INFORMATION I HAVE GIVEN IN THE FOREGOING APPLICATION IS TRUTHFUL, COMPLETE AND CORRECT, AND I MAKE THIS SOLEMN DECLARATION CONSCIENTIOUSLY BELIEVING IT TO BE TRUE AND KNOWING THAT IT IS OF THE SAME FORCE AND EFFECT AS IF MADE UNDER OATH.

_____
SIGNATURE OF THE APPLICANT

INTERPRETER DECLARATION

I,_____ , do solemnly declare that I have faithfully and accurately interpreted in the _____ language the content of this application and any related forms to the person concerned.

I have been informed by the person concerned, and I do verily believe, that he/she completely understands the nature and effect of these forms, and I make this solemn declaration conscientiously believing it to be true and knowing that it is of the same force and effect as is made under oath.

_____
(SIGNATURE OF INTERPRETER)

Declared before me at _____ this _____ day of _____ 19_____

_____
SIGNATURE OF THE OFFICIAL OF THE GOVERNMENT OF CANADA

Canadian High Commission  haut-commissariat du Canada

Canada

**Immigration Medical Division**
**Canadian High Commission**
**Macdonald House**
**38 Grosvenor Street**
**London W1X 0AA**

Service d'immigration

Fax: (0171)258 6506

REQUEST FOR POLICE CERTIFICATES/CLEARANCES

| FILE NUMBER: M95-2000 | SURNAME: |
|---|---|

**To Police or Relevant Authorities:**

The person who has completed the authorization form below is applying for admission to Canada as a permanent resident. To meet Canadian immigration requirements, each member of his/her family aged 18 years and over requires an original Police Certificate/Clearance of no criminal conviction.

We would ask that the Certificates be provided to the bearer of this letter, who will then forward them to the High Commission. If this is not possible, the Certificates should be sent directly to the High Commission, quoting the above File Number.

Thank you for your cooperation.

The High Commission

---

**TO BE COMPLETED BY APPLICANT**

**AUTHORIZATION BY VISA APPLICANT**
**FOR RELEASE OF POLICE AND COURT RECORDS**

I hereby authorize the Police or Relevant Authorities in _____(name country) to disclose any details of previous criminal convictions to the Canadian High Commission, London, England, for visa purposes only.

| SURNAME: | |
|---|---|
| **GIVEN NAMES:** | |
| **MAIDEN OR OTHER SURNAME(S) USED:** | |
| **NAME IN ORIGINAL SCRIPT (ie Arabic, Chinese etc):** | |
| **DATE & PLACE OF BIRTH:** | SEX: |
| **NATIONALITY:** | |
| **ALL ADDRESSES WHILE RESIDENT IN**_____(name country) | |
| **DATES** | **HOME ADDRESS** |
| | |
| | |
| | |
| | |

SIGNATURE OF APPLICANT:_____DATE:_____

Fig. 6. Request for police certificates/clearances.

40

**Citizenship and Immigration Canada / Citoyenneté et Immigration Canada**

**MEDICAL REPORT FOR CANADIAN IMMIGRATION**

**REF:M952000**

**DO NOT WRITE IN THIS SPACE**

**PLACE CASE LABEL HERE**

| 1. VISA OFFICE/CIC AND FILE NUMBER |
| --- |
| LONDON, UK |
| 2. I.M.S. SERIAL NUMBER |
| 3. FOSS CLIENT I.D. |

• PLEASE PRINT OR TYPE
SECTION A, BOX NOS. 4 TO 19 TO BE COMPLETED BY APPLICANT

**A. IDENTIFICATION OF APPLICANT**

| LAST NAME | | | GIVEN NAMES | | |
| --- | --- | --- | --- | --- | --- |

| DATE OF BIRTH | DAY | MONTH | YEAR | 6.COUNTRY OF BIRTH | 7.SEX | 8.MARITAL STATUS |
| --- | --- | --- | --- | --- | --- | --- |

| CITIZENSHIP | 10.COUNTRY OF PERMANENT RESIDENCE | 11.CATEGORY OF APPLICANT |
| --- | --- | --- |
| | | IMMIGRANT |

| 12. MAILING ADDRESS | 13. PROVINCE OF DESTINATION |
| --- | --- |

14. LENGTH OF STAY
PERMANENT RESIDENT

15. NUMBER IN FAMILY

AFFIX PHOTOGRAPH HERE.

NOT REQUIRED FOR INFANTS UNDER 18 MONTHS

TELEPHONE NUMBER

| 16. PRESENT OCCUPATION | 17. INTENDED OCCUPATION |
| --- | --- |

The remainder of this form is not to be completed without a photo of applicant

| 18. HAVE YOU BEEN PREVIOUSLY EXAMINED FOR IMMIGRATION TO CANADA? | YES | NO | IF YES, WHEN AND WHERE (CITY AND COUNTRY) |
| --- | --- | --- | --- |

19.PASSPORT NUMBER

NAME OF HEAD OF FAMILY

| FURTHER INSTRUCTIONS CONCERNING APPLICANT | SAWP | | CCP | | SR | | TREAT. | | DIS.DEP | | ADOPTION |
| --- | --- | --- | --- | --- | --- | --- | --- | --- | --- | --- | --- |

INSTRUCTIONS TO EXAMINING PHYSICIAN:

1. FORM NOT TO BE COMPLETED IF SECTION A NOT FULLY COMPLETED BY APPLICANT
2. PLEASE VERIFY THAT THE PERSON YOU EXAMINE IS THE PERSON DESCRIBED IN SECTION A. INDICATE DOCUMENT PRESENT FOR IDENTIFICATION AND ENTER DOCUMENT NUMBER.

| | PASSPORT NO. | | ID CARD NO. | | DRIVER'S LICENSE NO. | | OTHER (specify) |
| --- | --- | --- | --- | --- | --- | --- | --- |

ONCE APPLICANT IDENTIFIED, PLEASE APPLY DMP WET SEAL TO BOTTOM RIGHT HAND CORNER OF PHOTOGRAPH ATTACHED IN SECTION A ABOVE

3. ALL ITEMS IN SECTION B, D, E AND F TO BE COMPLETED BY EXAMINING PHYSICIAN.
4. DMP STAMP TO BE USED IN SECTION F.
5. APPLICANT TO SIGN IN SECTION C IN PRESENCE OF EXAMINING PHYSICIAN.
6. FEES RELATED TO THIS EXAMINATION ARE APPLICANT'S RESPONSIBILITY (UNLESS A LETTER FROM IMMIGRATION STATING OTHERWISE IS PROVIDED)
7. MEDICAL DOCUMENTS MUST NOT BE HANDED TO APPLICANT. IMM 1017 FORM, CHEST X-RAY, LABORATORY REPORTS AND IMMIGRATION APPLICATION MUST BE MAILED OR COURIERED IN SAME ENVELOPE BY EXAMINING PHYSICIAN'S OFFICE TO THE CANADIAN HIGH COMMISSION; IMMIGRATION AND MEDICAL DIVISION, 38 GROSVENOR STREET, LONDON, W1X 0AA, UK

**B. MEDICAL EXAMINATION (To be completed by examining physician based upon answers from the applicant)**

- This examination does not constitute immigration medical clearance.
- The medical examiner is asked to record any abnormalities found or any disease suspected. If some condition subsequently is disclosed which is not recorded on this form the applicant may be subjected to delay, removal from Canada, or other serious inconvenience.

HAS APPLICANT EVER SUFFERED FROM, OR BEEN TOLD HE HAD, ANY OF THE FOLLOWING CONDITIONS?

| | YES | NO | | | YES | NO | | | YES | NO |
| --- | --- | --- | --- | --- | --- | --- | --- | --- | --- | --- |
| 20. Nose or throat trouble | | | 30. Endocrine disorders | | | | 40. Other gastro-intestinal disorder | | | |
| 21. Ear trouble or deafness | | | 31. Malignant disorder or tumor | | | | 41. Kidney or bladder trouble | | | |
| 22. Chronic cough | | | 32. Mental disorder | | | | 42. Sexually transmitted disease | | | |
| 23. Asthma | | | 33. Head or neck injury | | | | 43. Genetic or familial disorders | | | |
| 24. Tuberculosis | | | 34. Hernia (rupture) | | | | 44. Operations | | | |
| 25. Other lung disease | | | 35. Rheumatism, joint or back trouble | | | | 45. Malaria (if yes, date of last attack) | | | |
| 26. High blood pressure | | | 36. Fainting spells, fits or seizures | | | | 46. HIV positive or AIDS (if yes, elaborate on reverse) | | | |
| 27. Heart trouble | | | 37. Typhoid or paratyphoid fever | | | | 47. Tropical deseases | | | |
| 28. Rheumatic fever | | | 38. Trachoma or other eye trouble | | | | 48. Alcohol and / or drug abuse | | | |
| 29. Diabetes mellitus | | | 39. Stomach pain or ulcer | | | | 49. Chronic skin condition | | | |

50. IS THE APPLICANT NOW TAKING ANY MEDICATION OR RECEIVING MEDICAL TREATMENT WHICH MUST BE CONTINUED IN THE FUTURE?   YES   NO
This is not a duplicate of any entry answered by the examining physician on the reverse. This question must be answered by the applicant.

51. HAS THE APPLICANT BEEN ADMITTED TO HOSPITAL OR OTHER INSTITUTION? (Other than childbirth?)   YES   NO
IF "YES" INDICATE:

| DATE OF ADMISSION | SYMPTOM / CONDITION / DIAGNOSIS | TREATMENT |
| --- | --- | --- |

**C. DECLARATION AND AUTHORIZATION OF APPLICANT (To be completed by applicant)**

I hereby declare that the information I have provided is true and completed. I authorize any physician, laboratory, clinic or hospital, to release to the Health Programs Directorate, any information concerning my health or medical history. I also authorize the Health Programs Directorate to release information obtained for the purposes of this immigration medical examination to a public health agency or a physician in Canada, if indicated.

| PLACE OF EXAMINATION | SIGNATURE OF APPLICANT (Signature of a parent or guardian is required if applicant is under the legal age) | DATE |
| --- | --- | --- |

IMM 1017 (3-94)E (M1-2-3)
LONDON MED1 (10/95)

# Canada

Fig. 7. Medical report for Canadian Immigration.

41

UPON MEDICAL EXAMINATOIN ARE THERE ANY ABNORMALITIES OF THE FOLLOWING

| | YES | NO | | YES | NO | | YES | NO |
|---|---|---|---|---|---|---|---|---|
| 52. Head and neck | | | 58. Chest, lungs and breasts | | | 64. Skin including surgical scars | | |
| 53. Mouth and throat | | | 59. Abdomen, liver, spleen, etc. | | | 65. Lymphadenopathy | | |
| 54. Ears | | | 60. Genito-urinary system | | | 66. Evidence of mental illness | | |
| 55. Nose | | | 61. Hernial sites | | | 67. Any other abnormalities | | |
| 56. Eyes including fundi | | | 62. Extremities and spine | | | 68. Female applicant pregnant. If yes, date of L.M.P. | | |
| 57. Heart | | | 63. Nervous system | | | 69. Is the applicant now taking medication, receiving or is expected to receive treatment of any kind | | |

| 70. HEIGHT | 71. WEIGHT | 72. VISUAL ACUITY (WITHOUT GLASSES) | | (WITH GLASSES) | | 73. HEARING WHISPERED VOICE 6 metres (20 feet) | | | |
|---|---|---|---|---|---|---|---|---|---|
| cm | kgm | R/6 | L/6 | R/6 | L/6 | RIGHT EAR | metres | LEFT EAR | metres |

| 74. BLOOD PRESSURE | IF ABNORMAL REPEAT B.P AFTER RESTING | 75. PULSE RATE (RESTING) | 76. PULSE RHYTHM | 77. MENTAL DEVELOPMENT | | |
|---|---|---|---|---|---|---|
| | | | | NORMAL ☐ | DULL NORMAL ☐ | BELOW NORMAL ☐ |

78. PLEASE ELABORATE ON ALL "YES" ANSWERS OR ABNORMALITIES 20 TO 77

79. CONCLUSION AND DIAGNOSIS

80. PROGNOSIS

E. LABORATORY FINDINGS (To be completed by examining physician) - ATTACH REPORTS, CHEST X-RAY, LABORATORY FINDINGS

81. ROUTINE BLOOD SEROLOGICAL TESTS FOR SYPHILIS (Candidates 15 years of age and older)

V.D.R.L.

F.T.A. - A.B.S. (or equivalent)
If applicable

82. URINALYSIS (Candidates 5 years of age and older)

| PROTEIN | SUGAR | MICROSCOPIC |
|---|---|---|

83. LARGE POSTERO-ANTERIOR CHEST X-RAY FILE AND RADIOLOGIST'S REPORT
(Required for all applicants 11 years of age and older)

CHEST X-RAY FILM NUMBER (if available)

F. IDENTIFICATION AND SIGNATURE OF EXAMINING PHYSICIAN (To be completed by examining physician)

NAME OF EXAMINING PHYSICIAN (Please print)

ADDRESS (Number, Street, City, Province, Country)

Postal Code

SIGNATURE OF EXAMINING PHYSICIAN

DATE

PLEASE ENSURE THE MEDICAL REPORTS AND IMMIGRATION APPLICATIONS ARE FORWARDED TOGETHER TO:
CANADIAN HIGH COMMISSION
IMMIGRATION AND MEDICAL DIVISION
38 GOSVENOR STREET
LONDON W1X 0AA UK

The **Immigrant Visa Processing Fee** is not refundable, regardless of the outcome of your application. The **Right of Landing Fee** is refundable if you are not issued a visa or if you withdraw your application. Fees must be paid by bankers' draft. Personal cheques are not acceptable.

You should be advised of the status of your application within twelve weeks. Hopefully, all will be in order and you will be issued your visa.

## SURVIVING THE INTERVIEW

An interview is not always required, but is at the discretion of your visa officer. Do not be alarmed if you are called to interview, it is not necessarily a sign that your application is in jeopardy. Quite the opposite, as the Immigration Division is very busy and not likely to waste time interviewing applicants who do not have a reasonable chance of being accepted. Often the interview is to determine the points to be awarded under the category of Personal Suitability.

If you are married your spouse will be requested to attend, along with any children over 18.

### Being assessed

What can you expect at the interview? As mentioned, your personal suitability will be assessed, as well as your professional qualifications. You can expect the visa officer to ask questions about your current job, past experience and education. Certainly he will want to know why you wish to migrate to Canada and what you have planned once you get there. You want to demonstrate a mature approach. Mention anything that shows you have thought the move through thoroughly and made contingency plans.

### Taking the opportunity to prove yourself

The visa officer wants to know that you will be an asset to Canada and that you will adapt well to life there. He will be looking for initiative, adaptability and resourcefulness. What he does not want to see is any evidence that you will not fit in or that you could become a drain on Canadian resources. This applies to all members of your family because, even if they are not accompanying you at this time, they may well do so in the future.

Don't be intimidated by the interview, which is held in a relaxed and informal manner. It is also your opportunity to ask questions, so be prepared if there is anything you want to know. In fact, asking a few questions is another way of demonstrating that mature and thoughtful approach the visa officer is looking for.

## COPING WITH OBSTACLES

Hopefully the process of obtaining the visa will be smooth, but if you run into problems or think your application may not be straightforward you might consider enlisting the aid of an immigration consultant or immigration attorney. These provide similar services, but you need to be aware of the differences, then decide which suits you best.

### Immigration attorneys

These are experts in the area of immigration law. They are governed by a professional watchdog body and provide a service for those who are having difficulties with their application, particularly applicants with past convictions or those who do not score enough points under the occupations category.

One of the key differences between an immigration attorney and a consultant is that only attorneys are allowed to attend immigration interviews. In a problematical case this could be very helpful and indeed comforting to the applicant.

*What will an immigration attorney do for you?*
Although firms vary, basically you are paying the attorney to provide legal advice and assistance in all matters pertaining to your immigration application. Most will:

- advise you on the best route to take for your application; for example, an applicant who is refused as a skilled worker may have stood a better chance under the Business Classification

- prepare your application forms and all supporting documentation

- train you for your interview

- attend your immigration interview, providing you with legal representation.

A major firm of immigration attorneys, Brownstein, Brownstein and Associates, warns that 'all too often the skills of an attorney are not called upon until an immigration application has been refused. It is always more difficult to reverse a negative decision than it would have

been to provide the best case possible with an attorney from the outset.'
If you feel you are likely to run into problems with your application,
that could be advice worth noting.

*Paying fees*
The scale of fees will differ from firm to firm, so ask for details when
you make contact. The address section gives a partial list of
immigration attorneys.

## Immigration consultants

These firms will help you with the immigration process but differ from
attorneys in that they cannot attend the immigration interview and are
obviously not as well placed to offer legal advice. However, they do
often include settlement advice and business services. Several also
assist with job placement. Enlisting the services of a consultant will
make things easier for you.

*Paying fees*
Balanced against that must be the cost which, again, varies from
consultant to consultant. Generally, the more services they provide the
larger the fee. See the address section for some immigration
consultants.

## The choice is yours

If, after carrying out your self-assessment, you think your application
will be pretty straightforward you may well choose to tackle the
procedure alone. If it doesn't look like plain sailing it could be worth
your while to pay an attorney or a consultant.

Do not be overwhelmed by all the rigmarole. In most cases it should
be pretty straightforward. And the good news is that during 1994 over
90 per cent of all skilled worker applicants successfully obtained their
visas. So it can't be all that bad!

## QUESTIONS ABOUT IMMIGRATION

1. *What is meant by the term 'skilled worker'?*

   This refers to a person with special occupational skills and
   experience which are transferable to the Canadian labour market.
   Refer to the Detailed General Occupations List to see the
   occupations that are acceptable.

2. *Will my professional/occupation qualifications be accepted in Canada?*

   Some will, some will not. Sometimes it is just a case of passing an examination or adding an additional qualification. It is up to you to find out if your qualifications relate to the Canadian labour market. You should contact a suitable professional body in Canada. Their names and addresses can be found in *The Canadian Almanac and Directory*. The Canadian Information Centre for International Credentials can also give information on this.

3. *One of my children is remaining in the UK. Does she still need to be included in my application?*

   Yes, if she is less than 19 years of age and unmarried at the time of your application.

4. *I have an aunt living in Canada. Will that help my application?*

   Yes, in that it will increase the number of points you are awarded. Remember that your relative must be over 19 and a permanent resident or citizen of Canada.

5. *I have heard that the procedure is different if I want to go to Quebec.*

   That's right, although it still follows the points system. You do not apply directly to the Canadian High Commission, but to your nearest Quebec Immigration Services office.

6. *Should I hire an immigration consultant or attorney? Will they help me to get my application approved?*

   That is entirely up to you. It is no guarantee of approval, but those who anticipate some difficulties might like to consider this option.

7. *Will I need to attend an interview?*

   That is at the discretion of your visa officer. If you are requested to attend, your spouse and dependant children aged 18 or over will be asked to accompany you.

8. *How long will it take for me to get my visa?*

   This is dependent on a number of factors, but the best way to ensure you get your visa quickly is to be certain you have enclosed all the relevant documents and information with your application.

9. *Will the Canadian Immigration Department help me to find a job?*

No. That is your responsibility. There are settlement services available, however, and you can find out about these from Canada Immigration Centres, Canada Employment Centres and placement professionals.

10. *Once I have immigrant status, how long does it last?*

You must proceed to Canada within one year of issue of the visa. Once there you will remain a permanent resident until you become a Canadian citizen or if you have frequent and/or lengthy absences from Canada.

11. *As a permanent resident, what exactly is my status in Canada?*

You and your dependants have the right to live, study and work in Canada.

You and your dependants are entitled to most social benefits. However, you cannot vote in certain elections and may not be eligible for some jobs that require high-level security clearances.

You are liable for Canadian federal and provincial taxes.

You or your dependants could be deported from Canada if you or they commit serious crimes.

## CHECKLIST

• Decide which immigration category applies to you.

• Study the points system. You need a minimum of 70 to be successful.

• Chances are you will need an approved, pre-arranged job in Canada to get a temporary permit.

• Students and young people looking for vacation work should contact BUNAC.

• It may be worth your while to enlist the services of an immigration attorney or immigration consultant. Consider this before making your application.

## CASE STUDIES

### Samantha is quietly confident

Samantha has contacted the Canadian High Commission and now has all the forms she will need to fill in. Initially she thought she would apply for a temporary work permit, as she only wants to go to Canada for a few years, but she soon realises that her best route is to go for Landed Immigrant status. Most temporary permits are only valid for a few months.

Working out her points for herself, Samantha is pleased to estimate them at 73. As a minimum score of 70 is needed, she is fairly confident and goes ahead with her application.

*Samantha's points*

|  | *Points* |
|---|---|
| ● Age: 24 | 10 |
| ● Education: BSc, Nutrition | 15 |
| ● SVP: Dietitian | 15 |
| ● Occupation: Dietitian | 1 |
| ● Arranged employment | 0 |
| ● Work experience (3 years since qualifying) | 6 |
| ● Language ability (fluent English, good A level French) | 12 |
| ● Demographic factor (set by federal government, assume 8 points for self-assessment) | 8 |
| ● Personal suitability (assigned by visa officer, assume 6) | 6 |
| ● Relative in Canada (none) | 0 |
| Samantha's self-assessed total | 73 |

### George runs into a problem

Although his points worked out at 77, more than enough to qualify, George encounters what could be a major difficulty with his application. Thirteen years ago, when he was 25, he foolishly drank too much at a party and was convicted of driving while under the influence of alcohol. He paid a fine and has not offended since but this appears on his police record. He contacts an immigration authority.

'Will that old offence seriously jeopardise my application?'

'I'm afraid it will,' the attorney replies. 'You need to apply for rehabilitation. It was a minor offence and quite some time ago, so we may be able to swing it.'

George hires the attorney, who undertakes the necessary legal work to have George 'rehabilitated'. He is successful in this (although the entire process takes nine months) and George is eventually granted Landed Immigrant Status.

*George's points*

|  | *Points* |
|---|---|
| • Age: 38 | 10 |
| • Education: HNC Electronic Engineering | 13 |
| • SVP: Electronic Engineer | 18 |
| • Occupation: Electronic Engineer | 5 |
| • Arranged employment | 0 |
| • Work experience (17 years since qualifying) | 8 |
| • Language ability (English only) | 9 |
| • Demographic factor (set by federal government, assume 8 points for self-assessment) | 8 |
| • Personal suitability (assigned by visa officers, assume 6) | 6 |
| • Relative in Canada | 0 |
| George's self-assessed total | 77 |

## Lucy gets a shock

Lucy assumes she will have no problem getting a visa because her Canadian aunt and uncle have offered to assist her when she arrives with temporary accommodation and help finding a job.

When Lucy calculates her points she is dismayed to learn that the help from her relatives is only worth 5 points to her, and as someone with no occupation and no experience she fails completely. She has no chance of getting a visa.

'Why don't you try contacting one of the outfits who help students and young people find temporary work in Canada?' the helpful immigration official suggests.

Lucy gets in touch with BUNAC and joins their Work Canada programme. This allows her aunt and uncle to support her application by undertaking to give her financial support if she runs out of funds or there is some other emergency. She discovers that she will also need evidence of a minimum of C$600 to support her job-hunting once she arrives in Canada.

Lucy finds temporary work as a waitress, with the intention of saving the C$600 as quickly as possible.

*Lucy's points (before applying to BUNAC)*

|  |  |
|---|---|
| • Age: 21 | 10 |
| • Education: 2 A-Levels | 10 |

# AM I ELIGIBLE TO APPLY FOR PERMANENT RESIDENCE IN CANADA?

| Factor | | Score | |
|---|---|---|---|
| 1 | Age | 10 | 10 |
| 2 | Education | 10 | 15 |
| 3 | Specific vocational preparation | 11 | 15 |
| 4 | Occupation (you must have at least 1 point here or arranged employment) | 10 | 15 10 |
| 5 | Arranged employment/designated occupation | 10 | 10 |
| 6 | Work experience (you must have at least 1 point here or arranged employment) | 6 | 2 |
| 7 | Language ability | 9 | 9 |
| 8 | Demographic factor (assigned by Immigration Division – for general self-assessment award yourself 8) | 8 | 8 |
| 9 | Personal suitability (assessed by visa officer – for general self-assessment award yourself 6) | 6 | 6 |
| 10 | Relative in Canada (bonus) (note that more than one relative in Canada does not result in more than the 5 bonus points) | | |
| TOTAL | | 80 | 85 |

Fig. 8. Immigration eligibility worksheet.

- SVP: none                                                          0
- Occupation: none*                                                  0
- Arranged employment                                                0
- Work experience*                                                   0
- Language ability: English and A-Level French                      13
- Demographic factor (set by federal government, assume
  8 points for self-assessment)                                      8
- Personal suitability (assigned by visa officer, assume 6)          6
- Relative in Canada                                                 5

Lucy's self-assessed total                                          52

*0 points in the occupation factor and/or the work experience factor automatically result in the application being rejected.

## DISCUSSION POINTS

1. You will need at least 70 points to get a visa as a skilled worker. Use the worksheet in Figure 8 to calculate your points. Do you have enough? If not, how could you increase your total?

2. Are your professional qualifications acceptable in the Canadian workplace? What will you need to do to 'translate' them?

3. Would it be worth your while to hire an immigration consultant or attorney, or do you think you can get your application through without help?

4. The immigration interview is designed to assess your suitability for Canada. They will be looking for initiative, motivation and adaptability. What sort of questions do you think they might ask? And what sort of answers should you give? Is there anything you would like to ask the visa officer?

# 3
# Choosing Location: Where to Work

## STUDYING THE GEOGRAPHY

Canada is a vast country, and there are enormous differences of climate, opportunity and lifestyle between the various areas. You may not be able to choose the location of your new job – you may already have an offer lined up, you may be being transferred by your firm or you may simply have already decided on the area that suits you best.

If not, it is worth taking time to look at what is available across the country. There are obvious factors to consider – if you are an avid skier you will not want to be knee-deep in grain fields in the heart of the Prairie Provinces! On the other hand, if you are an electronic engineer aiming to keep at the forefront of your technology, you need to head for an area of fairly intense industry such as Ontario.

The best way to get an overview of locale is to look at each of the ten provinces and two territories separately. The list that follows heads from east to west, and then up a bit to the Northwest Territories and the Yukon.

### Newfoundland and Labrador
- 405,720 square km
- population: 570,000
- capital: St John's
- other major population centres: Grand Falls and Windsor
- major industries: include fishing, mining, production of newsprint, oil and gas, hydroelectricity and tourism.

A maritime province consisting of two distinct geographical entities: Newfoundland and Labrador. The climate in Newfoundland is moderate and maritime with winters that are surprisingly mild by Canadian standards. Labrador has cold winters and brief summers.

**New Brunswick**
- 73,500 square km
- population: 723,900
- capital: Fredericton
- other major population centres: Moncton and Saint John
- major industries: include food and beverage manufacture, pulp and paper, sawmills, manufacture of furniture and other wood-based industries, metal processing, transportation equipment, processing of non-metallic ores and primary metals, tourism, fishing and agriculture.

A maritime province with a moderate and maritime climate.

**Nova Scotia**
- 55,491 square km
- population: 920,000
- capital: Halifax
- other major population centres: Sydney and Yarmouth
- major industries include: fishing and related industries, various manufactured goods, forestry, mining, offshore oil and gas production, tourism, agriculture.

A maritime province with a continental climate (defined as having vivid seasonal contrasts in which long, cold winters are balanced by mild to hot summers) somewhat moderated by the ocean.

**Prince Edward Island**
- 5,660 square km
- population: 130,000
- capital: Charlottetown, which is the only urban centre (62 per cent of the population live in rural districts)
- major industries: include agriculture, tourism and fishing.

A maritime province with a temperate climate.

**Quebec**
- 1,450,680 square km
- population: 6,895,963
- capital: Quebec City
- largest city: Montreal
- boasts a highly industrialised and diversified economy with well-developed agriculture, manufacturing and service sectors. Montreal

in particular is strong in space and aeronautics, telecommunications, energy and transportation.

An inland province almost entirely surrounded by water (Hudson Strait to the North, the St Lawrence River and Gulf to the south, James Bay and Hudson Bay to the west. Rather varied climate tending to very warm summers in the south and cold winters in both south and north.

## Ontario
- 1,068,580 square km
- population: 10,084,885
- capital: Toronto
- other major population centres: include Ottawa (federal capital), Thunder Bay, Kitchener, Hamilton, London, Sudbury
- major industries: a long list including automobile manufacture, diverse manufacturing, mining, forestry, finance.

It is worth noting that almost 80 per cent of Ontarians live in the southern half of the province, with most of the population in towns and cities near the US border. Ontario is Canada's most productive province, generating approximately 40 per cent of the country's gross domestic product.

An inland province bordering Hudson Bay in the north, with the Great Lakes and St Lawrence River in the south. An extremely varied climate, relatively temperate in the south and more severe east of the Great Lakes.

## Manitoba
- 650,000 square km
- population: 1,091,949
- capital: Winnipeg, where 60 per cent of the population live
- second largest city: Brandon
- major industries: initially based on agriculture, but manufacturing and transportation have increased greatly in importance in recent years; mining.

The first of the three prairie provinces as you travel west, Manitoba is one of the sunniest provinces in Canada. It has a continental climate with great temperature extremes (in Winnipeg, for example, the mean January temperature is -20°C, whilst the July average is about 19°C).

## Saskatchewan

- 651,900 square km
- population: 988,928
- capital: Regina
- other main city: Saskatoon. Together they are home to about one third of the population
- main industry: agriculture. Saskatchewan supplies 28 per cent of Canada's grain production
- other industries: include forestry and mining; research and development is a growing business with an emphasis on agriculture, space technology and biotechnology.

A prairie province, surrounded by land on all sides. Although winters can be harsh the whole province enjoys a hot, dry summer.

## Alberta

- 661,185 square km
- population: 2,545,553
- capital: Edmonton
- other main city: Calgary; more than half of Albertans live in these two cities
- major industries: one of the world's most productive agricultural economies, producing approximately 20 per cent of Canada's annual output; livestock production, mining, oil, gas production, forestry, food and beverage processing, production of petrochemicals and plastics, forest products, metals and machinery. The service sector is vital to Alberta's economy, accounting for over 50 per cent of the province's gross domestic product.

Two-thirds of all people in Alberta are under the age of 40, giving the province one of the youngest populations in the industrialised world.

The most westerly of the prairie provinces, with a continental climate. Seasonal contrasts are vivid and extreme resulting in long, cold winters and mild to hot summers.

## British Columbia

- 947,800 square km
- population 3,282,071
- capital: Victoria
- largest city: Vancouver, 60 per cent of the province's population live in these two cities

- major industries: BC's economy is based on the province's abundant natural resources; forestry plays a major role. Next most important economic sector: tourism, followed by mining of metals, minerals, coal, petroleum and natural gas. Agriculture and fishing are important areas. Manufacturing is still largely resource-based but is diversifying into telecommunications and the aerospace and subsea industries.

Vancouver is fast becoming 'The Hollywood of the North', with many major movies and television series being filmed there. Canada's west coast province. The climate is extremely varied, as is its topography. The coastal region is temperate with lots of rain and some snow; the interior has a continental climate. Other parts of the province could almost be described as desert-like, with extremely hot summers and equally cold winters.

## The Northwest Territories
- 3,426,320 square km
- population: 52,238, of whom most are Aboriginals (30,525) and live in small communities
- capital: Yellowknife, with the largest population at 15,000
- major industry: mining (valued at over $800 million)
- other industries: oil and gas exploration and development, tourism (the variety of landscapes offer superb fishing, wildlife observation and other outdoor activities).

Canada's most northerly territory, the Northwest Territories stretches from the 60th parallel all the way to the North Pole. There are two major climate zones: subarctic and arctic. Whereas the NWT enjoys between 20 and 24 hours of daylight in June it experiences up to 24 hours of darkness in December.

## Yukon
- 483,450 square km
- population: 27,797
- capital: Whitehorse, where almost 60 per cent of the population live, the rest spread out in small communities throughout the territory
- major industries: a small fishing industry in Dawson City; mining (more than 30 per cent of the economy); tourism plays a fairly large part; about 3 per cent of the population, mainly Aboriginal (who comprise 23 per cent of population), rely on the fur trade; agriculture is a small but growing industry.

The Yukon occupies Canada's northern west coast and has a subarctic climate. Much of the territory is at high altitude and consequently enjoys relatively warm summers. Winter temperatures average between 4 and -50°C in the south and colder still further north.

### Getting an overview

To complete your overview of the various provinces and territories, the chart in Figure 9 will give you a good idea of the temperature and precipitation variations across the country.

## LOOKING AT DIFFERENT LIFESTYLES

Although bare facts about climate, population and industry can give you a good idea of what the different areas are like, it is often the lifestyle you are really looking at. Let's look at the different regions again, but this time divide them into the seven generally accepted geographical regions, again working westward and then up to the north.

### The Atlantic Provinces: Appalachian Region

Referred to as The Maritime Provinces, New Brunswick, Nova Scotia, Prince Edward Island and Newfoundland are the smallest Canadian provinces and are all located on the east coast. Here the lifestyle is unhurried and uncluttered, the scenery magnificent and house prices low.

That said, the opportunities are limited for anyone in a high-tech profession. The fishing industry which once thrived is under serious threat from dwindling fish supplies.

### The Great Lakes: St Lawrence Lowlands

The major area to head for if your interests are industry and high-tech. Canada's capital, Ottawa, is located here, so it is the place for anyone wishing to work in government. Also in this region is Canada's largest city, Toronto, which is the home of the world's fourth largest capital market; Toronto's stock exchange is the second largest in North America by volume and third largest by value traded.

The lifestyle in the large cities is intense and bustling, although there is ample opportunity for leisure pursuits, with excellent sporting facilities and fine centres for arts. Housing in Toronto is difficult to find and expensive.

This area contains the majority of Canada's Francophone population and it would be foolish to attempt to settle in Quebec without an excellent command of French.

## TEMPERATURE AND PRECIPITATION AVERAGES BY REGION

|  |  | January | July | Yearly |
|---|---|---|---|---|
| *Vancouver (British Columbia)* |  |  |  |  |
| Temperature | Maximum | 5.7 | 21.7 | 13.5 |
|  | Minimum | 0.1 | 12.7 | 6.1 |
| Precipitation | Rainfall (mm) | 131.6 | 36.1 | 1117.2 |
|  | Snowfall (cm) | 20.6 | 0.0 | 54.9 |
| *Regina (Saskatchewan)* |  |  |  |  |
| Temperature | Maximum | -11.0 | 26.3 | 8.9 |
|  | Minimum | -22.1 | 11.9 | -3.8 |
| Precipitation | Rainfall (mm) | 0.5 | 58.9 | 280.5 |
|  | Snowfall (cm) | 19.2 | 0.0 | 107.4 |
| *Toronto (Ontario)* |  |  |  |  |
| Temperature | Maximum | -2.5 | 26.8 | 12.3 |
|  | Minimum | -11.1 | 14.2 | 1.9 |
| Precipitation | Rainfall (mm) | 18.5 | 76.6 | 664.7 |
|  | Snowfall (cm) | 32.3 | 0.0 | 124.2 |
| *Montreal (Quebec)* |  |  |  |  |
| Temperature | Maximum | -5.8 | 26.2 | 10.9 |
|  | Minimum | -14.9 | 15.4 | 1.2 |
| Precipitation | Rainfall (mm) | 20.8 | 85.6 | 736.3 |
|  | Snowfall (cm) | 47.7 | 0.0 | 214.2 |
| *Halifax (Nova Scotia)* |  |  |  |  |
| Temperature | Maximum | -0.3 | 21.8 | 10.6 |
|  | Minimum | -8.9 | 13.1 | 2.3 |
| Precipitation | Rainfall (mm) | 81.5 | 97.8 | 1178.1 |
|  | Snowfall (cm) | 48.9 | 0.0 | 192.6 |
| *St John's (Newfoundland)* |  |  |  |  |
| Temperature | Maximum | -0.7 | 20.2 | 8.6 |
|  | Minimum | -7.9 | 10.5 | 0.8 |
| Precipitation | Rainfall (mm) | 69.3 | 77.9 | 1163.1 |
|  | Snowfall (cm) | 83.0 | 0.0 | 322.1 |

(nb – all temperatures are shown in °C)

Fig. 9. Temperature and precipitation by region.

## The Canadian Shield
This area wraps around Hudson Bay and stretches east to Labrador, south to Kingston and northwest as far as the Arctic Ocean. Apart from the region of Kingston in the south, this is a low-tech area with a harsh climate and difficult conditions. The Shield has only a thin layer of soil and is definitely not the place for anyone keen on agriculture.

## The Prairies
'The grain bin of the world.' This is an apt description as the Prairies are comprised mainly of endless fields of wheat and canola that seem to go on for ever. But not only wheat is produced in the Prairies: Alberta is Canada's leading producer of petroleum, and much of the region contains deposits of oil, natural gas and potash. Technology and telecommunications are becoming increasingly important in the large cities. The winters can be bitter and the area is very far inland. Not for you if you have visions of sailing and surfing.

## The Cordillera
Where you will find the magnificent Rocky Mountains. Tourism is a major industry in these areas which include the world-famous ski resort, Banff. Not for you if you can't take the cold.

## The Pacific Coast
Sometimes known as Lotus Land, this is the destination of more immigrants to Canada than any other area. The temperature is the most moderate of all Canada's regions. People flock from all over the world to enjoy the many activities available on the west coast, from sailing on the Pacific to skiing in the Coast Mountains. The attitude to life here is pretty laid back – it is also called by some the California of the North.

Employment opportunities in Vancouver are quite good, although technology and industry are not as close to the forefront as in Toronto. Vancouver is a favourite destination for Chinese and Asian immigrants and the exodus from Hong Kong has vastly increased Vancouver's Asian population. Here you will find the famous Chinatown, second in size only to that of San Francisco. Due to the large influx of immigrants and the desirability of the area house prices are very high, particularly in Vancouver.

## The Arctic
This area is still largely populated by the Inuit (formerly known as Eskimos) and anyone thinking to move here would have to be made of

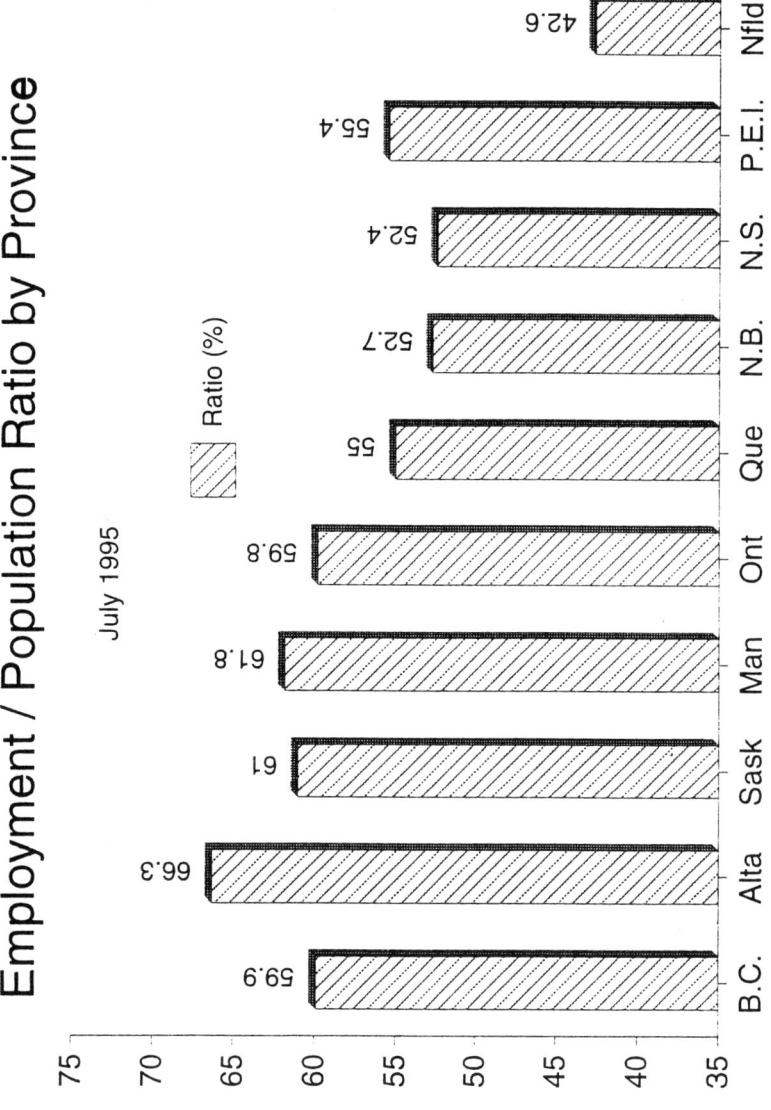

Fig. 10. Employment/population ratio by province.

similarly strong stuff. Although stunningly beautiful, the land is harsh with long, dark and bitterly cold winters.

## INVESTIGATING OPTIONS

Maybe you have already visited a part of Canada and decided that is where you would like to settle. It's a good idea to make sure that you will be able to get the sort of job you want there.

The various provincial tourist boards have a wealth of information about climate, geography and leisure activities and all are happy to send you a bumper pack of glossy brochures on request. Some have UK bases (see address section). As well as leisure-time information, many packs also contain valuable data about the industries in their areas.

### Looking at work opportunities

The following is a province-by-province look at growth in 1995, based on forecasts made in 1994 by the Conference Board of Canada. The percentages shown relate to real Gross Domestic Product (GDP) growth.

| *Province* | *Real GDP growth 1995* |
| --- | --- |
| British Columbia | 3.6% |
| Alberta | 3.3% |
| Saskatchewan | 2.0% |
| Manitoba | 3.5% |
| Ontario | 3.5% |
| Quebec | 3.2% |
| New Brunswick | 2.7% |
| Nova Scotia | 2.3% |
| Prince Edward Island | 3.1% |
| Newfoundland | 0.9% |

You are most likely to find employment in British Columbia, Alberta, Manitoba, Ontario and Quebec (see also Figure 10).

Obviously you will find the greatest choice and scope in one of the large cities, such as Toronto, Vancouver, Edmonton, Montreal and Quebec (fluent French speakers only for these last two).

### Finding work through newspapers

There is no national newspaper in Canada. Each of the major cities produces one or more papers which cater for that city and the surrounding area. Most will send you a recent copy on request (send an International Reply Coupon to cover postage) and from that you will be able to get a good idea of what the job situation is like in the area.

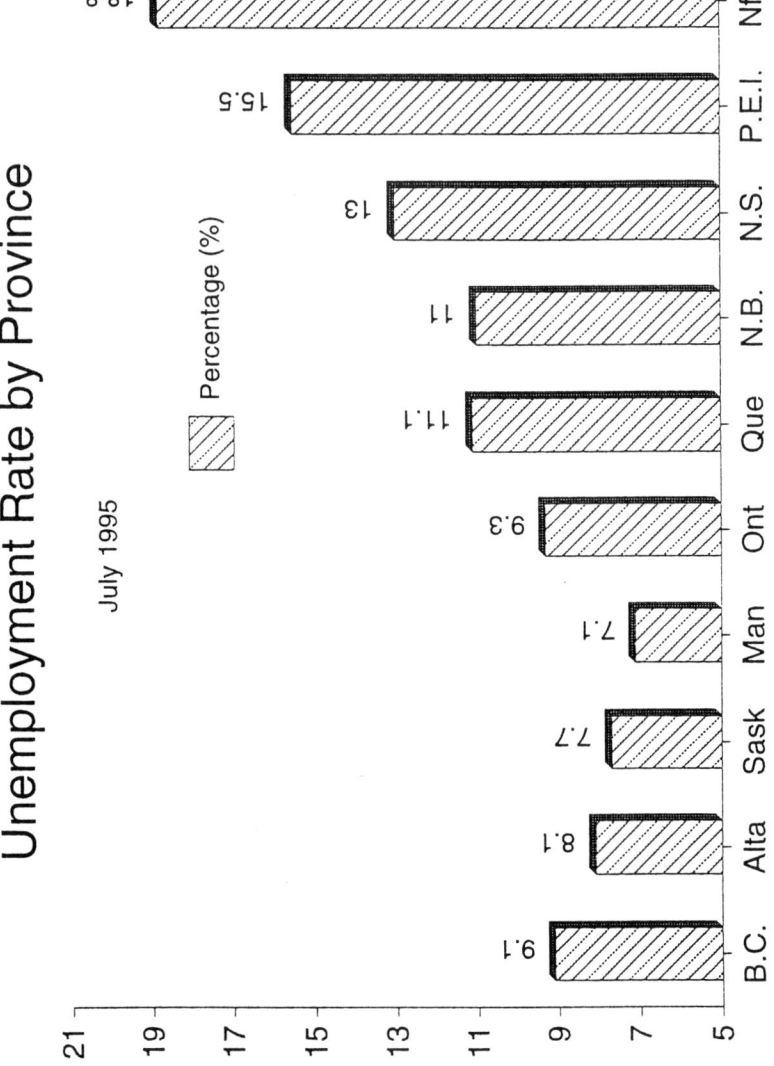

Fig. 11. Unemployment rate by province.

See Useful Addresses for details of the daily newspapers published in the major cities.

## Looking at wages and employment rates

Each province has set a minimum wage rate. These are currently:

| | |
|---|---|
| British Columbia | $7.00 |
| Ontario | $6.85 |
| Yukon | $6.72 |
| Northwest Territories | $6.50 |
| Quebec | $6.00 |
| New Brunswick | $5.50 |
| Manitoba | $5.40 |
| Saskatchewan | $5.35 |
| Nova Scotia | $5.15 |
| Alberta | $5.00 |
| Prince Edward Island | $4.75 |
| Newfoundland | $4.75 |

A major consideration when choosing location has to be the employment situation in that particular area. Figure 11 shows the unemployment rates in each province, as of July 1995. Look at this in conjunction with Figure 10 which indicates the number of people employed in each province relative to the population of that province.

## ESTABLISHING PRIORITIES

People make the decision to move to Canada for many different reasons. For some it is a question of lifestyle: others seek career opportunities; some are attracted by the wide open spaces. Unless you have already made your choice, or there are overwhelming reasons why only one area is suitable, it might be useful to use the following evaluation list to help you select an area, or a choice of areas – one of the appealing things about Canada is that there is a great deal to choose from.

## Ask yourself

1. What is my most important consideration – lifestyle or career?

2. What areas offer the work opportunities I need?

3. What areas offer the leisure activities I want?

4. Am I willing to make any trade-offs between the two?

5. Will the area I have chosen allow me to move forward in my career?

6. Do I mind being limited to one or two main industries or is a variety of opportunity important?

7. Am I looking for a metropolitan lifestyle or does something more isolated and rugged appeal to me?

## CONSIDERING THE FAMILY

The above list only looks at your personal preferences and considerations, which is fine if you are setting off on your own. However, if the family is coming along too there are a few other questions to ask.

1. Will there be opportunities for my partner to find satisfying employment, should she/he so desire?

2. If my partner is not planning to work in Canada are there enough leisure pursuits available? Will it be easy to meet and make new friends?

3. If children are accompanying you, would they be able to adapt to travelling fairly long distances to school or do you need to concentrate on an urban area with schools nearby?

4. Is anybody in the family sensitive to extreme cold? Or extreme heat? Both are facts of life in some areas.

## CHECKLIST

- Canada has many distinctly different areas with enormous variations in climate, geography and lifestyle.

- Seventy-six per cent of Canada's population of 27.3 million live in the major towns and cities.

- In parts of Canada you will need fluent spoken and written French to stand any chance of getting a job.

- The bilingual factor also applies if you wish to work for the federal government.

- Many areas, such as Vancouver, are temperate all year round. Others, like Ottawa and Toronto, experience cold winters and very hot summers. Be aware of these variations.

- Tourist boards are an excellent source of information about the different provinces and territories.

- There are no national newspapers. All the major cities are served by one or more local daily paper.

- The needs and wants of all accompanying family members are important when considering your intended location.

- Trade-offs between desired lifestyle and career opportunities may be needed.

## CASE STUDIES

### Samantha does some research

Sam's mum is still concerned about her daughter taking off to Vancouver.

'Will you be able to find work there? Do they have a hospital?'

Having visited Vancouver already, Samantha is convinced it is the place for her and is amused by her mother's attitude, as she knows Vancouver is a large cosmopolitan city with several hospitals, nursing homes and clinics.

'Mum, look at this information from the BC Tourist Board. See what a big place Vancouver is and how many hospitals and clinics there are just in the metropolitan area? There are several teaching hospitals, too. I'd like to work in one of them.'

Sam did some further investigation into the area she plans to move to, mainly to set her mother's mind at rest, but in so doing found out more about it for herself.

### George makes a plan

George and his wife realise that they need to know a great deal more about the different areas of Canada before coming to any decision about where to aim for.

'I wouldn't want the girls growing up somewhere where they have no access to culture,' his wife insists.

'But we do want some snow!' the children chime in.

'I think our major priority has to be the work situation,' George says.

George writes to the provincial tourist boards and receives packs of information. He realises that, as an electronic engineer, he will stand the best chance of finding employment in one of the major cities.

'Looks like Vancouver, Montreal or Toronto would be the best

places for us to start looking.' he decides.
'Not Montreal,' his wife points out. 'I don't think any of us have good enough French to be happy there, and you'd probably have a problem getting a job.'
The family is learning more about the country and beginning to identify the ideal area(s) for all of them.

## Lucy gets smart

Lucy's friend introduces her to a Canadian relative who is visiting.
'I understand you're hoping to work in Canada? Any idea where?'
'Anywhere will do. I just want to get away from this urban lifestyle. Somewhere with lots of trees will do.'
'In that case you've ruled out about half of Canada already,' the visitor smiles.
Lucy decides it might not be a bad idea to do a bit more research before she makes her plans. She studies the information sent by BUNAC and asks her relatives in Montreal to tell her more about the area where they live.

## DISCUSSION POINTS

1. What do you hope to gain from getting a job in Canada? Make a list of the benefits, as you perceive them, of making the move.

2. What are your priorities? Is your career the most important consideration or are you more concerned with general lifestyle?

3. Are you looking for an urban or a rural lifestyle? If the latter, do you have the skills and experience necessary? Would you and your family be able to adapt to a more isolated way of life?

4. Make a list of the areas in Canada where you are most likely to find demand for your skills. Make another list of those areas that most appeal to you from a recreational point of view. How do the two align?

5. Do you have friends or family in Canada? How important is it to live close to them?

6. After investigating the options, make a list of your top three destinations. Will you concentrate your job search in these areas, or are you willing to be flexible?

# 4
# Deciding on the Right Job

## GETTING TO KNOW WHAT IS AVAILABLE

Your choice of job in Canada may be obvious. If you are a qualified professional you will probably not be considering changing your career. However, even in this case you need to make sure that your British qualifications translate into Canadian equivalents.

If you are considering different options, there are many places from which you can get information about what is available. Firstly, there are quite a few publications which contain advertisements of positions available in Canada for workers from overseas. These include:

- *Overseas Jobs Express*
- *Canada Employment Weekly*
- *Canada News*
- *Jobs Overseas*
- *The Expatriate*
- *Careers International*
- *Graduate Posting*
- *Intel Jobs Extract*
- *Overseas Employment Newsletter.*

You will find further details of these publications and other job sources in Chapter 5.

The other important factor in your choice of job is immigration requirements, as dealt with in Chapter 2.

### Temporary and holiday work
If you are looking for a holiday job in Canada you will need to obtain temporary Employment Authorisation (a work permit). An organisation which specialises in helping young people and students to find temporary work and get a permit is:

BUNAC
16 Bowling Green Lane
London EC1R 0BD.
Tel: (0171) 251 0662.

They operate a reciprocal exchange programme called Work Canada. When you join BUNAC (current cost £4) they send you their *Job Seeker's Guide to Canada* containing all the information you need about finding a job, including applying for a work permit and making travel arrangements.

Other agencies which can help you find casual work or holiday work are listed in the Useful Addresses section.

Further information about temporary and holiday work can be found in various books, including:

* *How to Find Temporary Work Abroad*
* *Working Holidays 1996*
* *Summer Jobs Abroad*
* *Summer Jobs USA* (includes a section on Canada)
* *Working in Ski Resorts.*

## Exchange visits

This is an option for teachers wishing to take up work for a limited period in Canada. Teachers should contact:

The League for the Exchange of Commonwealth Teachers
Commonwealth House
7 Lion Yard
Tremadoc Road
Clapham
London SW4 7NQ.
Tel: (0171) 498 1101. Fax: (0171) 720 5403.

The role of this organisation is to:

* advertise for applicants for exchange

* select suitable candidates through application form and interview

* match the candidates with appropriate qualified overseas teachers

* negotiate exchanges with teachers, schools and employers

* confirm exchanges and provide a detailed service so that good

preparatory correspondence takes place about all professional and personal details including accommodation, travel to, from and within, visas, banking, medical care, cultural adjustment

• arrange a pre-exchange briefing conference and orientation conference

• offer full professional, social and pastoral service during exchange

• conduct debriefing and quality control exercises after exchange

• encourage and facilitate longer-term links.

The Canadian-based association which deals with education exchange visits is:

> Society for Educational Visits and Exchanges in Canada
> 57 Auriga Drive
> Nepean, ON K2E 8B2.
> Tel: (613) 998 3760. Fax: (613) 998 7094.

## Nannying

British nannies and au pairs are very well thought of in Canada. Several agencies will arrange placements for you; see the address section for details. Payment is usually in the form of accommodation and board, plus some spending money.

Canada Immigration currently requires that anyone obtaining Employment Authorisation to do this sort of work undertakes to remain in Canada for at least one year.

## LOOKING AT THE BUSINESS IMMIGRANT OPTION

As discussed in the chapter on immigration, there is another completely different route to working in Canada: as a self-employed person or entrepreneur. You will have read in that chapter what the necessary qualifications are for the Business Immigration Programme; if you fit the specifications and are interested in working for yourself there are quite a few factors to consider.

### Attracting the business immigrant

The Business Immigration Programme has proven very successful. In 1993 8,290 business immigrants landed in Canada, almost double that in 1991. That number continues to climb. What is the attraction for the businessperson and entrepreneur?

- Canada's wealth of natural resources means that energy is cheap.

- There is a sophisticated network of transportation systems, making goods easily available and facilitating distribution of your product.

- The work force is highly educated and provides another valuable resource.

- Canada has a proactive approach to taxation of Research and Development (R&D). Tax treatment of R&D is more favourable than in any other industrialised nation, including the US. One hundred per cent deduction for current R&D expenditure is allowed, as well as for capital expenditure on R&D machinery and equipment.

- The government is keen to encourage a successful environment for business and recently negotiated the North American Free Trade Agreement (Nafta) with the US and Mexico, creating a North American trading bloc of 360 million consumers, larger even than the European Union.

### Choosing the best areas

A recent study by *Report on Business* magazine identified the best cities in Canada in which to do business. They were:

- Saint John, New Brunswick
- Lethbridge, Alberta
- Winnipeg, Manitoba
- Ottawa-Carleton, Ontario
- Missassauga, Ontario.

According to the study these five showed 'the traits that business is currently looking for: dedicated, trainable workforces within short commutes; transportation routes or telecommuncations highways that afford easy access to markets; bottom-line advantages such as low labour and tax costs; infrastructure for telecommunications, pharmaceutical or engineering industries; universities with top research programmes; and pro-business attitude.'

Figure 12 shows the destination of Landed Business Immigrants in 1993.

| Province | Entrepreneurs | Investors | Self-employed | Total |
|---|---|---|---|---|
| Newfoundland | 5 | 1 | 1 | 7 |
| PEI | 2 | 6 | 3 | 11 |
| Nova Scotia | 343 | 68 | 57 | 468 |
| New Brunswick | 18 | 4 | 3 | 25 |
| Quebec | 1261 | 12 | 133 | 1806 |
| Ontario | 1057 | 691 | 543 | 2291 |
| Manitoba | 46 | 29 | 29 | 104 |
| Saskatchewan | 60 | 58 | 9 | 127 |
| Alberta | 348 | 126 | 81 | 555 |
| NWT | 2 | 0 | 1 | 3 |
| Yukon | 5 | 0 | 3 | 8 |
| BC | 1033 | 1646 | 206 | 2885 |
| Total | 4180 | 3041 | 1079 | 8290 |

Fig. 12. Destination of Landed Business Immigrants 1993.

**Finding more help**
Several organisations offer help and information for Business Immigrants.

*The Federal Business Development Bank*
This is a government agency formed to help promote and assist small business development and establishment. In Canada telephone 1-800-361 2126.

*The Ministry of Canadian Heritage*
They produce a directory of Canadian ethnocultural organisations which are specifically oriented toward business. The directory, called *Multiculturalism Means Business*, can be obtained by phoning 1-819-997 0797.

*Economic Development Departments*
The individual provinces offer an invaluable information service for business migrants in the form of brochures, seminars and counselling services. You need to contact the Economic Development Department of the province in which you are interested. Their addresses are in Useful Addresses.

## Being self-employed

If you do not intend to set up a business in Canada employing other Canadians, you still may be able to enter as a 'self-employed person'; the requisites for this category are detailed in Chapter 2. The official definition refers to someone who has the ability to purchase a business in Canada that will create employment for him/herself and make a significant contribution to the economy, cultural or artistic life of Canada. It includes farmers, artists, salespeople and those who can provide a specialised trade or service. Worth investigating if you prefer to go your own way. In 1992, 834 self-employed immigrants successfully used this alternative route, constituting 12.3 per cent of business immigrants in that year.

## ASSESSING YOUR CHANCES

If you have a British qualification in any profession you will need to find out how it translates into the Canadian market. Some qualifications will be acceptable as they stand, others will need to be augmented by further training in Canada or some sort of examination on arrival.

## Checking your credentials

If you feel this might apply to you, get in touch as soon as possible with The Canadian Information Centre for International Credentials. This is a very helpful organisation which assists individuals who want to know how to get their qualifications recognised in Canada. They do this by directing you to the appropriate regulatory body or professional association. Note that in Canada the assessment of foreign credentials and qualifications is done by professional regulatory bodies in each province. CICIC has a database of professional associations and provides information on the steps you will need to take to obtain recognition.

## Getting help with your check

There are credential evaluation services which provide an assessment of qualifications for general employment purposes. They will supply you with a letter of opinion regarding the value of your credentials. If you are a member of a professional body they will probably be able to advise you about the status of your qualifications in Canada. A fee is normally charged. These services are offered by:

Comparative Education Service
Room 202
214 College St
Toronto
ON M5T 2Z9.
Tel: (416) 978 2185
Fax: (416) 978 7022.

ICES
Open Learning Agency
4355 Mathissi Pl
Burnaby
BC V5G 4S8.
Tel: (604) 431 3054
Fax: (604) 431 3382.

Document Evaluation Service
York University
4700 Keele St
North York
ON M3J 1P3.
Tel: (416) 736 5217
Fax: (416) 736 5898.

International Credential
Assessment Service of
Canada Inc:

*British Columbia*
528 Carnavon St
New Westminster
BC V3L 1C4.

*Ontario*
111 Bond St
Toronto
ON M5B 1Y2.
Tel: (519) 763 7272
Fax: (416) 269 7612.

*Nova Scotia*
PO Box 226
Wolfville
NS B0P 1X0.

International Qualifications
Assessment Service
Alberta Labour, Professions and
Occupations
5 Floor
Peace Hills Trust Tower
10011–109 St
Edmonton
AL T5J 3S8.
Tel: (403) 427 2655
Fax: (403) 422 9734.

*For the Province of Québec only:*
Service des équivalences
Ministère des Affaires
internationales, de
l'Immigration et des
Communautés culturelles,
Direction des équivalences et
de l'administration des
ententes de sécurité sociale
360 rue McGill
Montréal
Québec H2Y 2E9.
Tel: (514) 873 5647
Fax: (514) 873 8701.

## FINDING OUT ABOUT PAY SCALES

The pay structure in Canada is roughly similar to that in Britain in terms of which jobs would be considered poorly paid, medium or well paid. However, salaries tend to be higher on the whole, particularly in the lower paid sections. The *International Pay and Benefits Survey* is a comprehensive guide to salaries around the world. It is available from:

> PA Personal Services
> Hyde Park House
> 60a Knightsbridge
> London SW1 7LE.

You can get an up-to-date and accurate idea of the going rates for various jobs by studying the advertisements and contacting employment agencies. There can be significant differences, depending on locale. Pay tends to be higher in the major cities, such as Vancouver, Montreal and Toronto where accommodation costs are high.

## MAKING CHOICES

A great many factors come into your choice of job in Canada. First and foremost will be the basis on which you apply for your visa. Study carefully the Occupations List at the end of this book. After that you need to look at what is available in the area you have chosen and how best you can fill that need. Will you, perhaps, come slightly downscale from your current career status in order to enter an industry that is growing and flourishing in Canada?

### The major industries

Here is a brief overview of the major industries, although it is worth remembering that almost any industry you can think of will be represented somewhere in Canada.

- Agriculture. In fact only seven per cent of land in Canada is arable, but Canada is one of the top exporters of cereal in the world.

- Fishing and fisheries. Canada is the world's leading exporter of fish and seafood.

- Forestry. A massive industry, but potentially troubled due to past over-exploitation of resources and current ecological concerns. Included under this heading is paper and pulp production which continues to flourish.

- Iron and steel. Manufacturing companies spread throughout many parts of Canada.

- Manufacturing. Includes food products, motor vehicles, electrical equipment, chemicals, textiles, aircraft, petroleum products, steel, aircraft and aerospace, industrial and agricultural machinery.

- Mining. Canada's mineral reserves are immense and include zinc, nickel, gold, silver, iron ore, uranium, copper, cobalt and lead.

- Petro-chemicals and gas. Canada is one of the world's foremost petroleum producers.

- Transportation. Understandably, in a country of this size, the transportation industry is very important. Development and manufacture of transportation equipment is a key area.

- Tourism. A growth industry, with more and more people from all over the world seeing Canada as an ideal holiday destination.

## CHECKLIST

- The Immigration Requirements are essential reading.

- You might qualify as a Business Immigrant or self-employed person.

- The various publications advertising jobs overseas are a good source of employment opportunities.

- If you are planning short-term employment contact an organisation specialising in vacation work, such as BUNAC.

- If you are a teacher an exchange visit may be appropriate. Contact The League for Exchange of Commonwealth Teachers.

- British nannies and au-pairs are highly sought after in Canada.

- You need to find out if your professional qualifications are acceptable in Canada and, if not, what you have to do to make sure they are. Your best contact is the Canadian Information Centre for International Credentials.

- Have a look at salary scales, bearing in mind that they vary according to locale.

## CASE STUDIES

### Samantha plans ahead
Samantha knows she wants to continue her career as a dietitian once she arrives in Canada, and it is on this basis that she intends to make her immigration application. However, she is concerned that her British qualifications may not be acceptable in Canada.

She writes to The Canadian Centre for International Credentials and discovers that she will have to undertake a short upgrading course. Fortunately, this can be done whilst she is still in Britain.

Samantha completes the course over the next two months on a correspondence basis. She is then given full accreditation when she applies to Canadian Immigration.

### George looks at his options
Fully trained as an electronic engineer, George specialised for some years in audio electronics.

'What I'd really like to do is get work in a recording studio, maintaining and upgrading the equipment. I wonder what sort of opportunities are available?'

'Perhaps you could write to some sort of association over there who could give you an idea?' his wife suggests.

George consults the *Canadian Almanac and Directory* and gets the addresses of the Canadian Academy of Recording Arts and Sciences and the Canadian Recording Industry Association.

As a result he gets information that indicates he may well be able to find work in that field, particularly in Vancouver or Toronto.

### Lucy is overwhelmed
Now that she has got into the idea of researching her future, Lucy is overwhelmed by the possibilities.

'I have no idea what I really want to do. I just wanted to get out of Britain. What shall I do?'

Lucy has a chat with a BUNAC counsellor, who is able to give her an idea of her options and recommends several books about temporary work abroad. After looking through these Lucy decides she would like to move around in Canada and identifies some possible temporary jobs that will allow her to do so.

## DISCUSSION POINTS

1. Will your chosen career get you the required points on the Immigration Selection Criteria? Do you have alternative skills and experience that might gain you more points?

2. Are you interested in short-term work in Canada? The people most likely to succeed in this area are teachers (exchange visits) and students/young people (vacation work).

3. What about the entrepreneur/self-employed option? Do you have money to invest in Canadian business? Do you have skills that could make a significant contribution to the economy, cultural or artistic life of Canada?

4. The self-employed alternative can be a bit chancy. Are you willing to take that risk? Do you have sufficient funds to support yourself (and your family) should your business take longer than expected to take off?

5. Are your professional qualifications acceptable in the area of Canada to which you are heading? If not, what will you need to do to bring them into line with local requirements? What can you do to set that process in motion before you leave?

# 5
# Starting the Search Before You Leave

## FINDING CONTACTS

To be realistic, unless you are going on a temporary working visit or are being transferred by your current company, you may not get a firm job offer before you leave for Canada. However, it *is* possible and greatly improves your chances with the immigration authorities as well as giving you a much less stressful transition. Where to start?

### Using publications

Why not start with the British newspapers? Most carry the occasional advertisement for jobs in Canada. The Sundays are your best bet.

Another possible source of Canadian job advertisements is professional journals, such as *Computer Weekly* or *The Economist*. If there is such a journal relevant to your occupation peruse it regularly.

### Specialist publications

There are specialist papers that carry advertisements for overseas jobs. One which concentrates wholly on Canada is:

> *Canada Employment Weekly*
> 15 Madison Avenue
> Toronto
> ON M5R 2S2.
> Credit card orders: Tel: (416) 964 6069. Fax: (416) 964 3202.

Also available from:

> Barkers Worldwide Publications
> 155 Mayberry Road
> Woking
> Surrey GU21 7JR.
> Credit card orders: Tel and Fax: (01483) 776141.

Current rates C$82.70 for twelve issues; C$25.00 for three issues. If ordered from Barkers £39.95 for twelve issues; £19.95 for five issues. A weekly publication; 52 pages including 300–400 job opportunities in Canada. When ordered from Barkers it is mailed in the UK the day before it goes on sale in Canada.

Another paper which carries advertisements for jobs all over the world, including Canada, is:

*Overseas Jobs Express*
Premier House
Shoreham Airport
Sussex BN43 5FF.
Credit card orders: Tel: (01273) 454522.

Current rates £18.95 for six issues; £29.95 for twelve issues; £52.00 for 24 issues. Published every two weeks; approximately 30 pages of advertisements for jobs all over the world.

Another publication which carries advertisements for jobs in Canada from time to time is:

*The Expatriate*
First Market Intelligence Limited
56a Rochester Row
Westminster
London SW1P 1JU.

Many of the advertisements in these publications are placed by agencies on behalf of their clients overseas, therefore it is worthwhile making a note of those agencies who recruit for your field of expertise.

A very helpful bulletin available from Canada is:

*Overseas Employment Newsletter*
PO Box 460
Town of Mount Royal
PQ H3P 3C7.

Another useful publication (although it does not contain job advertisements) is:

*Canada News*
Outbound Newspapers
1 Commercial Rd
Eastbourne
East Sussex BN21 3XQ.
Credit card orders: Tel: (01323) 412001.

Current rates £7.50 for six issues; £12.95 for twelve issues. A monthly publication containing articles about Canada, mainly concentrating on immigration, relocation and economics. An excellent source of advertisements for removal firms, immigration consultants, recruitment firms and more.

There are several other sources of advertisements available. The Canadian High Commission has a large selection of Canadian newspapers, magazines and journals and is happy to let you use its reading room. It is advisable to make an appointment.

The City of London Business Library also has a good range of Canadian publications:

City of London Business Library
1 Brewers Hall Garden
London Wall
London EC2V 5BY.
Tel: (0171) 638 8215.

A visit to your local reference library can be very productive. There you should be able to find the following three directories which list newspapers, magazines, journals and other publications throughout the world:

*Willings Press Guide*
*Benn's Media Directory*
*The Ayer Director of Publications.*

The *Directory of Jobs and Careers Abroad* is useful and can be found at many libraries.

*Publications for temporary work*
Several books contain worthwhile information and contacts, including *How to Find Temporary Work Abroad*, *Working Holidays 1996*, *Summer Jobs Abroad*, *Summer Jobs USA* (includes a section on Canada) and *The Directory of Summer Jobs Abroad.*

## Using agencies

Contacting employment agencies is possibly the best way of starting your search before you leave for Canada. There are many who deal with overseas placements but not all of them cover Canada. Listed in Useful Addresses are several which do; the list is by no means complete but is a starting point.

As mentioned, you can find out many of the agencies which make placements in Canada by perusing the advertisements in various publications. You can also look in *The Yearbook of Recruitment and Employment Services*, *The CEPEC Recruitment Guide* and *The Executive*

*Grapevine.* The Expat Network produces the *Canada Contact Directory* that gives the names, addresses and phone numbers of hundreds of recruiters. It costs £9.99 (includes p&p) and is available from:

Expat Network
International House
500 Purley Way
Croydon
Surrey CR9 4NZ.
Credit card orders by fax: (0181) 760 0469.

Your local library is likely to have the following directories which list agencies that make overseas placements:

*Directory of Executive Recruitment Consultants*
*Directory of Assessment and Development Consultants*
*The Directory of Canada Employment Agencies.*

*Looking at Yellow Pages*
A further source of employment agencies in Canada is the *Canadian Yellow Pages*: most city reference libraries have these for the major cities. However, there may not be a lot of point in contacting local Canadian employment agencies until you have arrived at your destination. The Association of Professional Placement Agencies and Consultants advised me that 'clients normally prefer to hire candidates who are immediately available to commence employment and therefore would be currently settled in Canada'. The spokesperson went on to say that where off-shore technical skills were sought, Canadian agencies would network with their counterparts in other countries. She finished by recommending that new arrivals contact the Association on their arrival, at which time they will redirect you to agencies within your field of expertise.

*Using employment consultants*
There are also employment consultants who will work with you more personally. Commonwealth Placements offer a wide range of services for those seeking employment in Canada, Australia and New Zealand. These services include:

● International Recruitment Programme. No charge to candidates; all fees are met by employers. Actively canvass on your behalf to find relevant vacancies and arrange interviews (sometimes by telephone or video-link).

- Commonwealth Jobsearch Programme. A fee is payable for this service, usually the equivalent of two or three weeks' wages. They will do quite a bit to help you find a job, including marketing your CV to potential employers, matching you with registered vacancies, letting you know of unadvertised jobs, coaching and tips on interview skills, resettlement advice and assistance.

These consultants can be contacted at:

Commonwealth Placements
Oxford House
College Court
Commercial Rd
Swindon
Wilts SN1 1PZ.
Tel: (01793) 535300. Fax: (01793) 542554.

A similar firm of consultants is The Oz Link. Although, as the name would suggest, initially established for those hoping to work in Australia and New Zealand, they now cover Canada as well.

The Oz Link
3 New St
Chulmleigh
Devon EX18 7DB.
Tel: (01769) 581318 (mobile 0374 159350).

*Professional placement agencies*
These often supply contact names and addresses of firms which are not actually advertising but who may have need of your particular skills and experience. Some that deal internationally may be able to help you with your search both before and after your arrival in Canada. Two such firms are:

Target Data Services Inc
2396–2398 Dunwin Drive
Missassauga, ON L5L 1J9.
Tel: (905) 858 7810. Fax: (905) 858 0112.

Dare Personnel Inc
275 Slater St, Suite 900
Ottawa, ON K1P 5H9.
Tel: (613) 238 4485. Fax: (613) 236 3754.
Internet: Dare@hypernet.on.ca

*Immigration consultants*
These often offer a complete service, including immigration advice and counselling. See Chapter 2 for more information.

With regards to temporary or holiday work, BUNAC is a very good option for young people and students.

Nannying is another possibility for temporary work, as are casual farm labour, work camps and temporary jobs for teachers. Some contact address are listed in Useful Addresses.

## Exploring other avenues

At this stage you are trying to spread your net as wide as possible. Some of the things you try may bear no fruit but, believe me, it is a fact that the more communications, feelers, applications that you can get out there, the more opportunities you will get coming back to you. Often a possibility will appear seemingly out of the blue and you will wonder why you sent out those dozens of letters to agencies and employers. But it is the constant outflow of queries from you that *leads* to that opportunity.

*Using contacts*
Make use of any and all contacts you can think of. If you have friends or family in Canada, write or phone them and let them know that you are on the search. Ask them to send you copies of their local papers (just the job section will do if postage becomes expensive) and enquire if they know of any job openings in their area. Perhaps they could get an application form from their place of work that you could fill in on spec. If you do something like that, be sure to mention your connection. Everything helps.

*Secondment or transfer*
Another possibility is secondment or transfer within the company you are currently employed by. This would only apply to a fairly large firm that has offices in Canada, but if this is the case make enquiries of your personnel officer. Beware though, if this approach comes to naught it could jeopardise your career path so only try it if you are committed to the move.

*Links Abroad*
Canada News operates a club called Links Abroad which is a contact base for anyone thinking of living or working abroad, as well as for those who have friends and relations abroad. As they put it: 'Specifically for people who have, or intend to have...links abroad'.

Whilst you may not directly find job opportunities through this association, it's all part of making contacts. And as a plus you will be eligible for lots of discounts all over the world, including special migrant airfares – very useful once you have succeeded in your job search!

*More ideas*

How else can you spread your net? There is always the option of placing Situation Wanted ads in Canadian newspapers and relevant journals. You can find the appropriate ones through the sources listed above.

Your professional body or trade union may be able to advise you of opportunities in other countries including Canada.

Several Canadian provincial governments have offices in the UK where you can usually find up-to-date listings of vacancies in the provinces served. Called Agents-General, their UK addresses are in Useful Addresses.

## World Wide Web

Don't forget the Internet. If you are not yet familiar with this source of information you will be amazed at what is available. It can be a bit daunting, though, as the data is all over the place. I recently saw the Internet described as being like a very large and very new library: full of all sorts of data but with no shelves or catalogues. Here are a few clues to help you start your search.

Human Resources Development Canada has several sites which provide labour market information including economic reports and reviews, labour force surveys and statistics. I have found the following locations:

• http://www.sunshine.net/www/200/sn0253/ecsrvmnx.htm for economic services reports

• http://www.the-wire.com.hrdc/hrdc.html for information from the Metro Toronto Canada Employment Centre

• http://canworknet.ingenia.com/canworknet

• http://www.hrdc-drhc.gc.ca/hrdc/ysc/yschomee.html for organisations developing working opportunities for young people

• http://www.scripps.edu/~xiang/job.html – a job-hunting guide for life scientists, but has a useful category called Other Directories of Employment Opportunities.

- http://www.islandnet.com/~cec5916 – will take you into information
  about BC job opportunities, but provides a link to the national Job
  Bank and to newsgroups posting jobs across Canada. It will also give
  information on how to apply for a Social Insurance number.

  Look out also for the newsgroups. For example, there is one called
  bc.jobs. Other provinces will have similar.
  Perhaps the best starting place of all is The Career Resource Home
  Page (http://www.rpi.edu/dept/cdc/) which gives a list of job databases
  and other employment related information on the Internet.
  You could even post a Situation Wanted type notice. Once again, the
  wider you cast your net the better! If you are not connected, you may
  have a friend who is. Ask her/him to guide you through. Or try your
  local library. Several city libraries now have Internet links which are
  available for your use and free of charge. You can usually find a
  computer-wise librarian to help you find your way.

## MAKING YOUR INITIAL APPROACH

### Replying to job advertisements
Let's look first at replying directly to companies that are advertising for
staff. How can you make your application stand out from the crowd?
Most important is a CV (or résumé) that really works. See the next
section for some tips. Of almost equal importance is your covering
letter. A CV is a fairly dry and blunt statement of your qualifications
and experience, but in the cover letter your personality and enthusiasm
should be apparent. Bear in mind, however, that a more formal style
will probably be appropriate if you are replying to a personnel office in
the UK; a lighter toned letter may be better suited if the application is
to be mailed directly to a Canadian address.

### Writing cover letters
Your cover letter should include information as to whether you have, or
have applied for, your Canadian Landed Immigrant Status or
Employment Authorisation. This information is important for the
employer, who needs some idea of when candidates will be available.
Give some indication of when you hope to receive your Authorisation
if you do not have it already.

*What to include*
Although the information will be in your CV, direct the prospective
employer's attention to any experience or training that is particularly

relevant to the position you are applying for. It doesn't do any harm to blow your own trumpet a bit! The great British art of the understatement is not understood or appreciated by most Canadians who tend more to the 'If you've got it, flaunt it' principle.

Employers usually appreciate a brief mention of how you came to know of the vacancy. Often they advertise in several publications and like to get an idea of which ones are working best for them.

*References and certificates*
References are not necessary at this point, although you will have mentioned in your CV that they are available on request. The same applies to educational certificates. However, you may feel that including these documents will add weight to your application, in which case it is perfectly appropriate to send copies at this point.

## Providing contact numbers

Particularly if you are applying to a Canadian address, a fax number at which you can be reached could prove useful. It could be to your advantage if an employer can reach you more quickly than another candidate. It is usually possible to 'rent' a fax address locally if you do not have a machine yourself. Look in *Yellow Pages* under Facsimile Bureaux and Secretarial Services.

Similarly, if you have access to the Internet an e-mail address could be advantageous.

*Checking your cover letter*
To sum up, you should try to include all of the following in your cover letter (whilst making it snappy and succinct!):

- Emphasise your suitability for the job, pointing out relevant experience and qualifications in your CV.

- State why you want this particular job.

- Give some idea of your availability.

- Include telephone number and fax number and/or e-mail address if possible.

- State how you became aware of the vacancy or (in the case of a speculative letter) the company.

- Try to include something that gets just a bit of your personality across.

A final note about presentation. If anything this is even more important when applying to a Canadian employer than it is with a British application. Use good quality paper, and a typewriter or printer that gives a dark and clean impression. If you do not have access to such equipment use a secretarial service. A small job such as cover letter and CV will not cost much.

## Contacting agencies

Much of the above applies to contacting agencies as well. One of the major differences is that they are likely to send you a comprehensive application form before going any further. A note on these: they are tedious and filling them in soon becomes a boring, repetitive task. Worse than that, the information asked for is invariably on your CV anyway! Resist the temptation to ignore them or to write See CV across the questions. Most agencies employ someone to input the data from these forms onto their database. That person is not employed to extract the data from your CV and, more importantly, might not put it in the form you want. So bite the bullet and fill in the forms as comprehensively as possible.

### Supplying references

An agency will probably also ask you at this stage for references. Although a name, address and telephone number might be sufficient for a UK-based agency it may not be appropriate for one based in Canada. Ask referees to write a reference for you in advance, addressed To Whom It May Concern. Send photocopies of these to the agencies, along with addresses and telephone numbers.

### The covering letter

Once again your covering letter is very important. If you are replying to an advertisement for a specific job you can follow the guidelines above, with an additional note about being interested in any other similar vacancies. If, however, you are contacting an agency to register with them and to be considered for any jobs in your field you will want to give a good idea of your experience and what sort of jobs you are qualified for and interested in. You may have skills that apply in several fields; be sure to point this out in your letter.

## WRITING ON SPEC

Yet one more way to cast your net wide is to write speculative letters to companies which might need your skills. Most of these cold contacts will elicit no response, but there is always the possibility that your letter and CV will arrive on the personnel officer's desk on the very day that she despaired of ever finding the right person to fill that post which you were obviously born for.

Look for large companies that may require your expertise. If your field is administration your target area will obviously be pretty broad. If your skills are more specialised you will find fewer prospective employers to write to but will probably have a better chance of hooking one.

### Using libraries for contacts

If you are able to get to London the best place to find the names and addresses you want is the City Business Library, the address for which is given earlier in this chapter. They have the *Yellow Pages* for all cities and towns and you will find more addresses than you can ever want.

Any fairly large city library will having listings of Canadian companies. Ask the reference librarian – they are invariably helpful. In particular look out for the *Canadian Key Business Directory*, published by Dun and Bradstreet, which gives a profile of the top Canadian firms and includes names, addresses, telephone numbers, and the names and titles of executives who run each company. It also contains a useful geographical listing. Consult also the *Canada Business Directory*.

### Contacting international companies

A good speculative approach is to contact British companies which have branches in Canada, as well as Canadian firms with branches in the UK. This removes the possible obstacle presented by the great distance between you and your prospective employer. This can be one of the best ways to find a job before applying for Employment Authorisation, thus greatly enhancing your chance of getting immigration approval. There is an excellent directory published by Dun and Bradstreet, *Who Owns Whom*, which gives you this information and which you should find in almost any reference library.

Following this tack of contacting international companies, you could try contacting the Chambers of Commerce listed in the address section that may provide you with lists of British companies in Canada and Canadian companies in Britain.

## Writing the cover letter

When making speculative enquiries your cover letter is possibly more important than the CV itself. Follow the general rules stated above but emphasise the trumpet-blowing even more. You really are selling yourself, and doing it cold which, as any salesman will attest, is the hardest thing of all. You need to tailor your letter to the type of firm you are writing to as well as to the sort of job for which you are looking.

## TURNING A CV INTO A RÉSUMÉ THAT WORKS

Although we have been referring to CVs, the term in use in Canada is Résumé. Although similar to a CV, a résumé differs slightly in both format and content. Figure 13 shows a typical Canadian-style résumé. A CV tends to include more personal details than you will find on a résumé.

### Types of résumé

You have a choice of type of résumé. Figure 13 shows the chronological résumé. Figure 14 is an example of the functional résumé, which categorises your experience into areas of skill and expertise. The chronological résumé is the usual form but either will be acceptable and you should choose the one that best highlights your abilities and suitability. You may wish to draw up one of each sort and decide which is most appropriate for each application.

Note that both examples cite a Job Objective. This is not absolutely essential and appears to be an American innovation. However, Canadian employers are becoming increasingly accustomed to seeing this on résumés. This is certainly an area in which you can customise your résumé for optimum results.

### 'Tweaking'

Which brings us to a very important point: tailoring your résumé to fit the job for which you are applying. If you have access to a word processor this need not be an onerous task. It really is worth taking the time to check your résumé each time you send it out, to see if it really shows off the skills required for a specific job. It is largely a question of emphasis. Say, for example, that you are applying for a middle-management position with a firm that manufactures and supplies surgical equipment to doctors and hospitals. You do not have experience of this product, but your management skills are exemplary. You would 'tweak' your résumé so that even greater emphasis was given to these assets. You would also mention the

Résumé of
Jeffrey Gilbert

123 Green Lane
Godmanchester
Cambs PE18 3TR
United Kingdom
Tel: 44-1480-388678
Fax: 44-1480-388542

JOB OBJECTIVE: R&D Manager

## EMPLOYMENT

| | |
|---|---|
| Date: | 1990 to the present. |
| Employer: | Inx Printing Technologies plc, St Ives, Cambs, UK. Design and manufacture of industrial ink jet printers. |
| Position: | Research and Development Group Leader Project management, staff placement and supervision, budget preparation and finance control for the group. Technical involvement in all aspects of the projects. Long-term product planning. Other responsibilities include patent preparation, quality issues, and deputising for the Director. |
| Date: | 1986 to 1990. |
| Employer: | Neve Electronics Ltd, Melbourn, Herts, UK. Design and manufacture of audio recording consoles. |
| Position: | Planning Manager Planning, monitoring and progressing company-wide product development programmes. Project planning encompassed all stages of product development from concept to customer training across all departments. Development of long-term planning strategies for R&D, manufacturing and sales. Responsibilities included budget preparation, staff placement, work scheduling and project expenditure. |
| Date: | 1978 to 1986. |
| Employer: | DA Jet Ltd, Cambridge, UK. Design and manufacture of industrial ink jet printers. |
| Position: | Project Manager Preparation and management of both short- and long-term product development strategies. Responsible for coordination and management of project resources and administration of engineering budgets and schedules within R&D. Senior design authority, responsible for engineering standards and project development equipment. Staff supervision and placement (20 plus). |

Fig. 13. Chronological résumé.

| Date: | 1974 to 1978. |
|---|---|
| Employer: | Roband Electronics Ltd, Crawley, Sussex, UK.<br>Industrial and military power supply manufacturer. |
| Position: | Senior Design Engineer.<br>Design of industrial and military power supplies and fail-safe control systems to military standard 05-21.<br>Research and development of switching converters.<br>Prototype development supervision, and production liaison. Environmental testing and field trials supervision. |
| Date: | 1970 to 1974. |
| Employer | General Post Office (Telecommunications Division), UK.<br>Telecommunications. |
| Position | Technical Trainee.<br>Apprenticeship in electrical and electronic engineering.<br>Various work assignments throughout the G.P.O. Block release to Openshaw Technical College. |

## EDUCATIONAL ATTAINMENT

1971–1974     Openshaw Technical College, Cheshire, UK.
HNC in Electrical and Electronic Engineering.

1965–1971     Long Road Secondary, Sale, Cheshire, UK.
General Certificate of Education A-Levels (equivalent to post high school diploma) in Maths, Electronics, Physics and Telecommunications.

## ADDITIONAL COURSES

| 1983 | Microprocessor Applications |
|---|---|
| 1989 | 'C' Programming |
| 1992 | Electro-Magnetic Compatibility |
| 1993 | Basic Company Finance |
| 1994 | Total Quality Management |

## ADDITIONAL INFORMATION

Member of the Institute of Patentees and Inventors.

With over twenty years' experience in the electronics industry, I have developed a broad knowledge base in both engineering and project management. Because of my knowledge of other disciplines such as mechanics, pneumatics, and fluidics, I can apply my problem solving abilities to most areas of a project. This is particularly valuable in project management roles.

# RÉSUMÉ

## JOHN CROSS

728 Whitehorse Lane
Brentford
Middx TW8 0NY
United Kingdom
Tel: 44-0181-476 8665
Fax: 44-0181-476 0967

**JOB OBJECTIVE:**
Senior Sound Engineer or Producer of various forms of popular music, including dance, rock and easy listening.

**ENGINEERING EXPERIENCE:**
Senior Engineer at Blue Moon Recording Studio, London, UK. Worked on CD albums released by chart-topping GirlzOwn and Mandy White.

Engineer at SuperSound Studio, London, UK. Responsible for pre-mixes.

Apprentice Engineer at Roll 'Em Studios, Lincoln, UK.

**PRODUCTION EXPERIENCE:**
Producer at Pinewood Studios, Manchester, UK. Produced various artistes including Conqueror and Fave-Rave. Produced and mixed the top twenty CD album 'My Little Unicorn' by the Triplettes.

**EDUCATION:**
Higher National Diploma (equivalent to post high school diploma) in Sound Recording and Production Services, Sinclair School of Sound, Lincoln, UK.

General Certification of Education O-Levels (equivalent to high school diploma) in Maths, Design and Communication, English, Photography, Science.

**OTHER DETAILS:**
Member of the Association of Professional Recording Services. Fully computer literate with experience of various graphic and audio software programmes.

Fig. 14. Functional résumé.

voluntary work you did at a blood donor clinic. If the firm supplied food products the latter would be irrelevant, although you would still emphasise the former.

## Explaining terms
When listing your qualifications remember that some letters and designations may mean nothing to the Canadian employer. If you are a MICE by all means say so, but write it as Member of the Institute of Civil Engineers. Similarly some educational terms may be unknown. For example, A-Levels do not exist as such in Canada. So list them, but put in brackets 'equivalent post-high school diploma' or something similar. O-Levels or GCSEs would be 'equivalent to high school diploma'. Most university-level degrees translate well, although different classes of degree should probably be spelled out.

## Leave no gaps
Just as you want to draw attention to the high points of your education and career, you do not want your potential employer focusing on the difficult areas. Most of us have something in our career past that looks a bit odd or needs explaining – gaps in employment, for example. Try to limit the negative impact and even, if possible, turn it into something positive.

### Explaining employment gaps
Do not leave employment gaps unexplained or try to cover up the fact. If you were looking for a job, say so. If you did any training during that period, be sure to point it out. That illustrates a proactive approach. Or if you took some time out to travel the world, say just that. The recruiter may admire your spirit of adventure! At least he won't be imagining you spending a year as a couch potato.

### Explaining education gaps
Gaps in your education can cause a problem too. Perhaps you began a degree course but did not complete it or gain the qualification you were studying for? Should you omit the fact or give details and risk having the prospective employer think you a failure? It is possible to make a plus point of even this. Outline what you did achieve (*eg*, first year BA Business Studies) and, if possible, any plans you have to complete the course. Whatever you do, don't leave a gap. As with the employment gap, the recruiter will wonder what you were doing for two years and may well come up with something less favourable.

*Explaining career changes*
Another potential problem area is frequent career changes. There is a fine line between being perceived as a flexible go-getter or as shiftless and unreliable. If you have moved about quite a bit during the course of your career there is no disguising it. Try instead to highlight other areas which might reinforce your reliability and commitment – for example completing a long degree course or having held positions of responsibility. Do not try to explain the frequent changes by complaining about the companies for which you worked. That just makes you seem a moaner.

## Effective presentation
Once again, presentation is all important. You want to make a good job of selling yourself, but not at the risk of the recruiter losing interest. A résumé for someone with ten to 20 years' experience will likely run to two pages. More than that is not advisable. If you really do have a long list of credentials and experience you may need to resort to providing a one-page summary followed by the more detailed version, but in almost every case two pages should suffice. Those with shorter careers to date should try to get it all on one page. What you *don't* want is one-page-and-a-bit! Either squeeze it into one or elaborate to two full(ish) pages.

Even though you are probably going to be sending the résumé and letter by air mail, don't go for lightweight paper. A good, heavy bond gives a subconscious and immediate impression of reliability and solidity. What was said earlier about the cover letter applies even more to the résumé itself. The type must be bold, clean and clear. Photocopies are acceptable as long as they are of good quality. You might even like to jazz the whole thing up by using a coloured paper; nothing too garish, but a very light blue or buff will make your résumé stand out from the rest without shouting.

*Your résumé checklist*
It is not possible to overstate the value of customising your résumé to fit the job applied for, so not all of the above will apply in each case. You should, however, be sure to include the following on every résumé:

● Name, address and telephone number. Fax number and e-mail address if applicable.

● Full details of your educational attainment. Be sure to translate your qualifications into terms understood by Canadians, if necessary.

- Details of your career to date. Give names of employers and dates, and outline your duties and responsibilities.

- Other relevant information such as membership of professional associations, public offices held and other skills. There is excellent scope for 'tweaking' in this area.

## IMPRESSING THE CANADIAN EMPLOYER

If you do all the above you will impress any employer! But what we want to look at here is your impact specifically on the Canadian employer. It is true that most Canadians love all things British, so play on that. It is one of your assets. Although you want to avoid the great British understatement, a little bit of British eccentricity might not go amiss. Just a touch, mind! Do not attempt this if you are applying to a Francophone company.

### Overcoming competition
You will often be competing with resident Canadians for a position. What you can offer that they cannot? In addition to a bit of 'Britishness' you have one other inherent asset. You are obviously adventurous and not frightened of new challenges, otherwise you would not be attempting to embark on a career in a new country.

The other side of the coin is that a prospective employer could wonder if you are going to stay the course; are you going to get fed up with Canada and wander off? The way around that is to emphasise your intrepid and flexible nature whilst indicating your commitment to your new life in Canada. Canadians are susceptible to flattery regarding their country so you could say something complimentary about Canada and how much you are looking forward to being part of its growth.

### Selling yourself
What exactly is the Canadian employer looking for?

- experience
- training and education
- confidence
- enthusiasm.

Additionally, a second language is a great asset. A good command of French is vital if you choose to work in either a Francophone area such as Quebec or in government. Other languages are useful too due to Canada's multicultural nature. If you are thinking of getting a job in Vancouver, for example, Cantonese would help tremendously. The most important message as far as getting a job in any part of Canada is concerned is *sell yourself*. Let employers know what you can do for them. Highlight your assets and skills. Do something to make yourself stand out from the crowd. Present your experience as favourably as possible. If you are used to living and working in Britain that may not come easily, it isn't the British way. But it *is* the Canadian way and you need to get a handle on it in order to succeed.

## CHECKLIST

• The British newspapers will occasionally have advertisements for jobs in Canada.

• *Canada Employment Weekly* has extensive listings for job opportunities in Canada.

• *Overseas Jobs Express* carries ads for jobs world-wide, including some in Canada.

• *Canada News* has articles of real interest to those planning to move to Canada.

• *The Canada Contact Directory* is a very useful guide to employment agencies which recruit for Canada.

• Some British firms have offices in Canada, some Canadian ones have branches in the UK. These are ideal targets for your speculative letters.

• You might consider using the services of a recruitment consultant, such as Commonwealth Placements.

• Make use of all your contacts, including friends and family in Canada.

## CASE STUDIES

### Samantha gets a job before she leaves

Sam decides she would like the security of having a job lined up in Canada before she leaves, not least because it would put her mother's mind more at rest!

She decides to invest in the services of a professional placement agency. Through the *Overseas Jobs Express* she locates one that specialises in placing health personnel. For a fee they put her in touch with the Burnaby Outpatient Clinic, which is looking for a consultant dietitian. CV, educational certificates and references are sent. Finally the placement agency arranges for an on-line video interview.

'Good news, Mum. You don't have to worry any more. I've got a job lined up, just outside Vancouver.'

'Will you have to travel far? In all that snow?'

Some mothers will worry about anything, but at least Samantha is set!

## George sets his search in motion

George realises that the chances of getting a definite job offer before he arrives in Canada are slim, but wants to set the search in motion.

'Aren't you spending a lot of money on all these subscriptions?' his wife asks.

'An international job search is bound to take some money, but it will pay off in the long run. These publications will be useful to me once we arrive in Canada, too. And the sooner I put myself into the job market, the better.'

George is being realistic. An international job search *does* use up resources – both time and money – but he is going about it exactly the right way.

## Lucy casts her net wide

Lucy has joined BUNAC and read several very helpful books about finding temporary work abroad. She realises that she can do more by making use of her contacts in Canada. She writes to her aunt and uncle to ask them to keep an eye out for any opportunities in their area.

Her uncle writes back. 'Bob's Burger Bar just down the road from us is going to be taking on extra help come June. That's when their busy season starts. I mentioned you to him – told him you were arriving in May. He's going to hold a place open for you provisionally. It's not much, just waitressing, but it will be something to start you off.'

Lucy is well on her way to a successful working tour of Canada.

## DISCUSSION POINTS

One of the key messages of this chapter was *sell yourself*. That isn't always easy. You need to do it in a way that suits you, to be comfortable with it. If blowing your own trumpet does not come easily to you, try the following:

1. Have a look at your experience, including your education. What are the high points? What do you have that makes you better than the next applicant?

2. Having identified your strengths, think about how you can put them across. If you are someone people feel comfortable talking to, for instance, that will not be apparent from your CV. You will have to make a point of it if it is relevant to the job you are applying for. How can you do that? Have you perhaps been involved in some voluntary work that makes it obvious, or will you have to be bold and just state the fact?

3. Get a friend to help now. Ask him to pretend that he does not know you, then give a one- or two-minute speech that outlines your career and experience. Try to accentuate all your positive assets, but tell the truth about your accomplishments. When you have finished, your friend should tell you what he has learned about you from your precis. Compare that with what you both know about your skills and experience. Then try it again, with even more emphasis on the positive.

Before you can start selling yourself you need to make contacts.

4. Which job sectors are you interested in? Which agencies deal with placements in these fields?

5. Have a look at the advertisements in the overseas jobs papers. Are any close to your skills and interests? Are they placed by agencies or individual companies? If agencies, you can contact them for similar opportunities. If individual companies, you could write a speculative letter asking if they have any openings in your field.

6. Do you know anyone who lives in Canada, or anyone who knows anyone who lives in Canada? Can you take advantage of this contact?

7. Think about tailoring your CV/résumé for different opportunities. Could you cut the work involved by having one generic résumé and three or four variations?

8. How can you make your résumé and cover letter stand out from the crowd?

9. Most Canadians love all things British. How do you feel about trading on that? Would you be embarrassed?

# 6
# Arriving in Canada

## SETTING OUT

You have your visa, you know where you're headed, and you either have a job lined up or a good idea how to go about getting one and enough resources to keep you afloat while you search. Time to set out. The preparations you will need to make depend on your personal circumstances and whether you are heading to Canada for good or for a limited period. In either case there are some essentials to be sorted before you leave.

### Banking arrangements

Be sure to inform your UK bank of your move. You may decide to keep the account going for a while, even if you are permanently relocating to Canada. It is a good idea to do this, as UK payments frequently need to be made after you have been away for a few months or more and it is easier to do this from a UK account. If you do decide to close the account make sure you clear any direct debits or make alternative arrangements for paying them.

Make sure you are taking sufficient money to tide you over until you are fully settled in. Travellers cheques are best for ready cash. If large sums of money are involved (say, the proceeds of the sale of your house) it is best to let the UK bank know that you will shortly be requesting transfer of the funds. Once you have started an account in Canada you will advise them of the details and the money will be transferred.

It's a good idea to ask for a letter of introduction from your bank. This will make opening an account in Canada simpler.

### Tax and National Insurance

Inform the tax office of your move. There will be adjustments to be made in the form of a rebate or tax owing by you. If you have been self-employed, or had any significant income from sources other than regular employment, it is worth hiring an accountant to sort out your accounts before you leave. If there are any queries it is so much easier to deal with them from the UK. Similarly you will need to inform the Social Security office of your plans. You should contact:

Department of Social Security
Overseas Branch
Newcastle upon Tyne NE98 1YX.
Tel: (0191) 225 7341.

Be sure to take any relevant tax and National Insurance documents with you to Canada, including your National Insurance number.

## Tidying up hire purchase arrangements

Make sure that these are all up to date and either make final payments or arrangements to continue your payments from Canada. (This is one of the instances when it is simpler to maintain your UK bank account for a while.)

## Arranging insurance and pensions

You will need to sort out any insurances: medical, life, property *etc*. If you are going to Canada as a permanent resident you will be eligible for provincial insurance cover on, or shortly after, your arrival. However, you should take out some travel insurance before you leave to cover the journey and the period before registering. If you are on a temporary visit you will definitely need some medical coverage. You will find that the provincial medical insurance cover in Canada is quite good (similar to the NHS) but you may wish to retain private insurance. In this case you will need to find out if the policy you currently hold will be applicable whilst you are in Canada.

Contact the administrators of any pension plans you contribute to and discuss future arrangements.

Contact your car insurers and get some sort of record of your claims history, otherwise you may well find yourself paying full premiums if you are unable to prove any no claims history.

## Redirecting subscriptions and mail

Make sure you have either cancelled or redirected any subscriptions and make arrangements with the Post Office to have your mail redirected. It is advisable to pay to have your mail sent on for at least a year. Even if you think you have informed everybody you know of your new address, it is easy to miss somebody. You wouldn't want the letter from long-lost Great Aunt Gertrude's solicitor informing you that you have inherited her fortune to be returned Address Unknown!

## Utilities

If you are making a long-term or permanent move be sure that your gas, electricity and phone bills are paid up. If your move is short-term make suitable arrangements for temporary disconnection or redirection of statements.

## Selling or letting your home

There are many variables here; you may be selling your house before you leave or may intend to rent it out. If you are renting it try to arrange for someone to keep an eye on the property for you. Your best bet would probably be to put it in the hands of an accommodation agency as then you will not have to worry. Some mortgage companies, though, do not take kindly to you letting your property. Some simply disallow it and others insist on very expensive insurance. Even those who are fairly amenable to the idea can take a very long time to give their approval.

## Taking pets

If you are travelling to Canada for a few months only you will probably not be taking your pets. Although they can enter Canada without too much trouble they will have to spend six months in quarantine in Britain on your return. If your move is more permanent you may well want to take them with you. In that case you will require a certificate from a vet stating that they are in good health and fully up to date with all their vaccinations. You will also require an export licence which can be obtained from:

> The Ministry of Agriculture
> Hook Rise
> Tolworth
> Surbiton
> Surrey KT7 6NF.
> Tel: (0181) 330 8183.

There are several firms that specialise in relocating pets; you would be well advised to deal with them. They can advise you on all the requirements and make sure that your pet is as comfortable as possible. A partial list of these firms is in Useful Addresses. Or you might just like to ask your vet, who may be able to advise you of a suitable local firm.

Additionally, some moving companies offer a pet travel service. These include Davies Turner Worldwide Movers and TCP Worldwide Freight Services Ltd. (Addresses in the general list of removal firms in Useful Addresses.) Other removal companies may also offer this service; enquire when you contact them regarding your move.

## Taking your car

Although it is possible to ship your car to Canada, in most cases it really isn't worth it. It will have to undergo fairly stringent testing to see if it complies with environmental and legal specifications, and will probably cost you much more than if you just sell it and buy another in Canada. You would also have the nuisance of having your steering wheel on the wrong side of the car as Canadians drive on the right.

## Voting rights

You will retain your right to vote in British elections (as long as you remain a British citizen) even if you remain in Canada for some time. Contact the Electoral Registration Officer in your local district for more information. Be sure to register with the nearest British Consulate on arrival in Canada.

## Taking your belongings

Not much to worry about if you are only going for a month or two. For a more permanent move, though, you will no doubt want to take considerably more of your belongings. Think about what you *really* want to take with you, as furniture is generally of good quality and not particularly expensive in Canada. You may find that your existing furniture does not fit well in the usually larger Canadian home and there is the expense of shipping it.

There are many reputable firms of international movers. Useful Addresses has a list of those contacted during the writing of this book which offered a comprehensive service to Canada. The addresses given are for their head offices; most have branches all over the country. A quick look in your *Yellow Pages* will lead to many others. Contact several firms, as charges and services vary; all should supply free quotations. It's a very competitive market, so use that to your advantage.

### Customs requirements

You will be allowed to import your personal possessions into Canada without paying duty. You can get full details of your entitlements from the Canadian High Commission. Also, your removal firm may be able to provide you with the necessary forms and help you complete them, if required. It is very important to make a detailed list of all personal/ household items that you are bringing with you, as well as items that may follow later. You will be required to produce two copies of this list for Customs and Immigration on arrival in Canada.

## Your document checklist

As well as making all these arrangements you need to be sure to take all the official documentation you may require. Here is a short checklist of what you will need; it probably should end with 'anything else you can think of'!

### Driving licence

You can drive in Canada on your UK licence for a year, so there seems little point in bothering to get an International Driving Licence. If you do want one, though, contact the RAC or AA. At the end of the year you will need to take a Canadian driving test. These are administered and issued by the provincial governments. You are unlikely to find the test onerous as the examiners tend to realise you are an experienced driver – they just like to make sure that you are aware of local regulations. After passing this test you will be issued with a provincial driving licence. A warning: in most provinces you will be asked to surrender your UK licence! So if you think you are likely to need that again, make a note of the number before you hand it over to facilitate replacing it on your return to the UK.

### Certificates

Take all your educational certificates, including any for training courses. Photocopies will not be sufficient in some cases. You will also need to take originals of such documents as birth certificate, marriage licence, certificates of adoption and so on.

### References

As mentioned elsewhere, it is a very good idea to gather as many written business and personal references as you can before you leave. It is not easy for a prospective employer to telephone a referee in the UK. The same applies to landlords, who often require personal references. So get everyone you can think of to write something nice about you. When you show these recommendations in Canada make sure you keep the original.

### Medical records

Visit your doctor before you leave and ask for some sort of basic record of immunisations, hospitalisations, allergies *etc*. Get something similar from your dentist, and give these to your new doctor and dentist in Canada.

### Passport

One Year Visitor's passports are not valid for entry into Canada so be sure you have a full passport. It's also a good idea to renew your passport if it is due to expire in the next few months – it's simply easier to do so whilst in the UK. Passport application and renewal forms are available from main post offices.

*Visas*
Make sure you have your visa tucked away safely with your passport as you will need to show it on arrival.

## Thinking about your move

Even if you have visited Canada before, or have friends or relatives there, there will inevitably be a period of readjustment. For a time it might all seem a bit confusing. Some of this disorientation can be avoided by finding out as much about your destination as possible. As well as looking at some of the publications and books listed in the Further Reading section at the end of this book (many of which you will be able to find in your local library), a visit to the Centre for International Briefing in Surrey might be worthwhile. There you will find a very good library containing all sorts of information on lifestyle, conventions, regulations and laws in various countries. They do charge a fee.

Moving Publications Ltd is another useful source of information on specific areas of Canada. They publish a series of magazines targeted at people relocating to eight major areas in Canada, with information about real estate, cost of living, utility costs, municipal laws, transportation, education, pretty much everything you could need! The guides cover Alberta, Vancouver and BC, Montreal, Ottawa/Hull, Winnipeg and Manitoba, Toronto and Area, Saskatchewan, Greater Hamilton and Area. The 1995 price was C$7.95 plus C$6.00 handling charge for one guide and C$3.00 for each additional guide if you order them from Europe.

## TAKING CARE OF ESSENTIALS

### Finding accommodation

Your first concern on arrival will be accommodation. If you are fortunate you will have friends or relatives who will put you up for a while. If you have been transferred by your UK firm they may have arranged accommodation for you. Failing that you will need to have sorted something out for at least the first week or so.

*Locating temporary accommodation*
Bed and breakfast type accommodation is available in most towns and cities and might be your best bet on arrival. Better still, arrange it

before you leave. Contact the Better Business Bureau in the city or the city nearest the area you are moving to. See Useful Addresses for a list of the bureaux in major cities.

A book entitled *B&B in the US and Canada* lists many of these establishments. It costs £6.50 and is available from bookshops (you'll probably have to order it) or you can get it from Canada News mail order service for £7.50.

Goodies
Canada News
1 Commercial Rd
Eastbourne
East Sussex BN21 3XQ.
Credit card orders: Tel: (01323) 412001.

Cheques/postal orders crossed and payable to Outbound.

*Locating permanent accommodation*
Once you have a temporary roof over your head you could contact a rental agency to get something more permanent. That's where the letters of recommendation you brought with you will be useful as landlords are very keen to have some evidence of your reliability before letting the accommodation. You will also need to be prepared to pay at least one month's rent in advance, as well as a security deposit usually equivalent to one month's rent in the case of furnished accommodation. After that you may wish to begin looking for a house to buy. The procedure is much the same as in the UK, except that agents tend to cover a much wider area in Canada, where they are called **real estate agents**. You will also find that you get a more comprehensive service from your agent, who will usually accompany you to homes that you wish to view and will be able to provide you with a good deal of information about the property before you see it. Although this varies from province to province, you are likely to need at least a five per cent deposit, in most cases ten per cent.

## Making health care provision
Health care is another provincially regulated area. The cost of medical treatment in Canda can be high if you have not applied for government sponsored health insurance. Do this as soon as possible on your arrival, if you are eligible. Application forms for health insurance, and other information, are available at Canada Employment Centres or through the provincial Department of Health. In some provinces there is a waiting period or a time limit in which to apply for early coverage.

You should also find a doctor and dentist as soon as possible. These are listed in *Yellow Pages* under Physicians and Surgeons, Dentists, and Clinics-Medical. If you have friends or relatives in the area ask for recommendations. Be sure to ask if the doctor belongs to a provincial health insurance plan. If not, you will pay a great deal more for your health care. You should also compare the rates charged by dentists, as there is no universal dental insurance, although many employers offer a group plan. Take the records you brought with you from your UK doctor and dentist to your new practitioners.

**Transportation**

Most cities are fairly well served by public transport, but Canadians do rely on their cars pretty heavily, particularly in more rural areas. Unless you are in a big city you should probably think about getting some sort of personal transport as quickly as possible, otherwise your job search may be hampered. Car lots proliferate in most areas and good deals are to be had on second-hand cars.

## REGISTERING WITH SOCIAL SECURITY

Another top priority. Although you have a work permit you will not be able to start employment without a Social Insurance Number (SIN). *Yellow Pages* again: your local Canada Employment Centre will be found under the Government Services listing. It's a pretty straightforward process: you just fill in a few forms outlining your work background, and some personal details, and you are then issued with a SIN card (see Figure 15 for an example). Be sure to take this with you when you attend interviews.

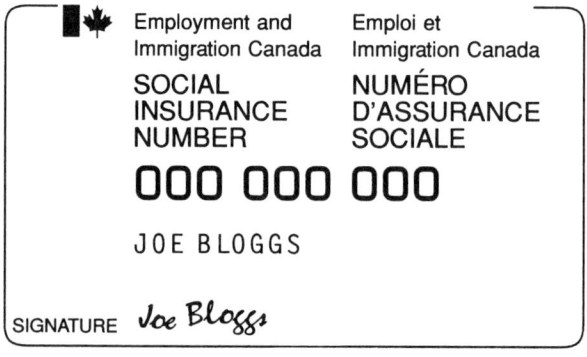

Fig. 15. Sample Social Insurance Number card.

As well as being the place where you register for your SIN the Canada Employment Centre is an extremely good source of information and assistance during your job search. It offers the services of government advisers, has extensive job listings and a wealth of publications, directories and lists that you can make good use of.

## FINDING OUT WHERE TO LOOK

You are now set up and ready to begin the job search in earnest. Where to look? It is all a lot easier now that you are actually in your chosen locality. As mentioned you can get help from the Canadian Employment Centre.

### Reading the local papers
The next step is to get hold of all the local papers, both daily and weekly, and scan the jobs section. Figure 16 shows examples from several major cities. Make it your priority every day to scan these advertisements and get your applications off as quickly as possible. Sometimes a job advertisement will invite you to ring for an informal chat about the position. Do so. Anything that helps to make you memorable is to the good, and this gives a proactive impression.

### Making speculative approaches
The procedure is not very different from conducting the search from the UK – just easier. Consult *Yellow Pages* for firms which seem to be in your field and send them all a speculative letter. Stress your versatility and adaptability and that you are available to start immediately.

*Using libraries*
Your local library will have addresses and telephone numbers of Canadian companies arranged by job sector: for example, manufacturing, retail, service. Make use of these. As in the UK librarians are usually very keen to help, so if you let the reference librarian know what you are after and why, you will get all sorts of useful information. As in the UK the use of public libraries in Canada is free. The library will have a full selection of newspapers covering all of Canada. The Wednesday and Saturday editions usually carry the most job adverts.

Whilst in the library consult *Matthews Media Directory* for listings of daily newspapers, business and trade publications and news, satellite and wire services. Also try *Matthews CCE Directory*, containing listings for community papers, the ethnic press, multicultural radio and TV stations as well as the university newspapers and radio stations.

Fig. 16. Sample Canadian newspaper advertisements.

Some of the publications featuring job vacancy advertisements are:

- *Canada Employment Weekly*
- *Jobs, jobs, jobs*
- *National Business Employment Weekly.*

*Finding the right publication*
Job-specific magazines which carry advertisements for vacancies include:

- *CA Magazine* (for chartered accountants)
- *Canadian Music*
- *Canadian Nurse*
- *Explore*
- *Marketing Magazine*
- *Medical Post*
- *Northern Miner*
- *Pulp and Paper Canada.*

*Checking the notices*
Still at the library, you can check the bulletin board to find out what is available to job-seekers in your area. You might be able to:

- join a job-finding club

- offer your skills on a voluntary basis

- attend relevant lectures and job fairs

- join a professional development association.

By doing any of these you begin to immerse yourself in the community and create your own network of contacts.

## Finding leads from other sources

If you have friends or relatives in your new location they might be able to introduce you to someone from their firm, or they may have other influential contacts. Don't be afraid to ask.

Human Resources Development Canada, a government body, produces various newsletters and info sheets which can be a valuable source of information about the Canadian job market. Ask at your Canada Employment Centre.

Yet another source of contacts and information is the Canada Career Information Partnership (CCIP), a national network of government and private sector agencies which provide career and labour market information to Canadians. See Useful Addresses for contact details.

If you have the use of a computer with a modem attached you can access Community Nets and Freenets, of which there are more than 60 in existence or being organised throughout Canada. These electronic networks provide local information, a place for interest groups to hold discussions, e-mail service for individuals and limited access to the wider Internet. Here are the telephone and modem numbers for some of these in the major cities.

| Location | Name of Service | Office # | Modem # |
|---|---|---|---|
| Calgary | Calgary Free-Net | 403 220 8914 | 403 282 4075<br>403 282 3707 |
| Edmonton | Edmonton Freenet | 403 421 1745 | 403 428 3929 |
| Vancouver | Vancouver FreeNet | 604 257 3811 | 604 257 8778 |
| Victoria | Victoria Free-Net | 604 727 7057 | 604 479 6500 |
| Winnipeg | Blue Sky Freenet | 204 992 4357 | 204 987 1234 |
| St John's | St John's InfoNET | 709 737 4594 | 709 737 3425 |
| Halifax | Chebucto Comm. Net | 902 494 2449 | 902 494 8006 |
| Ottawa | Nat'l Cap Freenet | 613 788 3947 | 613 564 3600<br>613 564 0808<br>613 564 0670 |
| Toronto | Toronto Free-Net | 416 979 9242 | 416 780 2010 |

## VISITING AGENCIES

Employment agencies are the other avenue to explore. Most cities have them in abundance. Your first step is to identify those which recruit in your field of expertise, and then blitz them with your letter and résumé. Be prepared for a lot of foot-work, as most will want you to come for a personal interview before putting you on their books.

### Looking for the right agencies

As in the UK some agencies are better than others. Look for those that seem to be interested in you personally. In fact, an agency that doesn't want a personal interview probably isn't going to come up with much to help you. Be sure that you let them know exactly what you are looking for; you don't want to waste your time and travelling expenses attending interviews for inappropriate jobs.

Keep up the pressure. Most agencies deal with hundreds, if not thousands, of job-seekers in a month. It is easy for a consultant to remember somebody he saw yesterday, but he may forget you if you were last in touch three weeks ago. Make it part of your routine to phone them regularly, drop into their offices if you are in the vicinity. Make yourself memorable so that they remember you when the good job comes along.

For help in finding the right agencies for you, contact:

> The Association of Professional Placement Agencies and Consultants
> 114 Richmond St East
> Suite L-109
> Toronto
> ON M5C 1P1.
> Tel: (416) 362 0983. Fax: (416) 360 5478.

They will direct you to appropriate agencies within your field of expertise. If you are looking for a temporary placement contact:

> The Federation of Temporary Help Services
> 409, 1 Eva Road
> Etobicoke
> ON M9C 4Z5.

## CHECKLIST

Before you go you will need to:

- Tidy up all your administrative and personal affairs.

- Be sure you have original copies of all important documentation including educational certificates, birth certificates, marriage licence.

- Contact several removal companies and get quotations. Find out exactly what services they offer and get a firm price.

- Get personal and business references in writing.

- Get evidence of your automobile insurance no-claims history.

- Remember passports and visas.

After you arrive in Canada you will need to:

- Contact a Canada Employment Centre to register for employment and get your Social Insurance Number.

● Register with the Provincial Health Plan, if you are eligible.

● Find a suitable doctor and dentist.

● Start scanning the classified ads in daily and local papers.

● Contact the Association of Professional Placement Agencies and Consultants to find suitable employment agencies.

● Check the local *Yellow Pages* for employment agencies and possible employers.

● Send out an avalanche of applications, speculative letters and letters to employment agencies.

## CASE STUDIES

### Even Samantha doesn't always get it right!

It looks as if Sam has everything under control; she has upgraded her qualifications and even secured a Canadian job before leaving England. She has tidied up her affairs in the UK, arranged temporary accommodation in Vancouver and now arrives in Canada.

On the way from the airport to her bed and breakfast the taxi is involved in a slight accident. No one is seriously hurt, but Sam has bumped her head and the taxi driver insists on driving her to hospital, just to check for concussion.

'You have got travel insurance, haven't you?' asks the taxi driver.

'No. I understood I'd be covered by the BC Medicare Programme,' replies Samantha.

'Not until you've registered with the Plan,' says the receptionist in accident and emergency.

As a Landed Immigrant Samantha would indeed be eligible for the provincial health insurance scheme, which would have covered her in this emergency. However, it is not automatic and she does need to complete all the necessary forms. She should have arranged some temporary travel insurance.

### George continues his search

George and his family have settled in Toronto. As soon as they arrive George continues his search.

At the reference library he finds a wealth of contacts and information about the Toronto area, much more than he was able to get hold of while still in the UK. He consults *Matthews Media Directory* which leads him to a couple of publications specialising in the recording industry. George puts together individualised résumés and speculative letters for the studios mentioned in these publications.

Within ten days he has been invited to three studios to chat about possibilities.

## Lucy is off to a good start

Lucy's aunt and uncle meet her plane. She is thrilled to finally be in Canada (even if she can't see much in the way of wide open spaces around the Montreal airport!).

'We'll stop at Bob's Burger Bar on the way home, Lucy,' says her uncle. 'He's anxious to meet you. I hope it's not too much of a rush, but he's kind of hoping you could start tomorrow. They're rushed off their feet.'

Lucy's aunt intervenes. 'That's ridiculous. She'll still be jet-lagged. And beside, she's got to register with the CEC first. He can't pay her if she doesn't have a SIN.'

Lucy is fortunate to have a relative to guide her through the formalities of registering with a Canada Employment Centre and getting a Social Insurance Number.

## DISCUSSION POINTS

1. There are a lot of details to take care of before you go. Make a list of everyone you deal with on a non-personal basis (banks, hire purchase companies, tax authorities *etc*). Who needs to be informed of your move? What information will they need from you? Compile your own checklist and work steadily through it.

2. Do you have all the documentation you need to take with you? Is anything missing? What will you need to send for?

3. Who could provide you with a written letter of recommendation? Consider employers and friends. Have you done any voluntary or community work in the past?

4. What do you need to do to prepare for your arrival? Have you arranged satisfactory temporary accommodation?

5. How will you arrange your job search once you arrive at your destination? You might devise a daily schedule with a list of priorities.

# 7
# Applying for Jobs

## DECIDING ON AN ANGLE

Once you have located a job possibility you still have to compete with many other suitable applicants. You have to stand out from the crowd and that means finding an angle.

### Finding your assets

You already have an advantage in that you may be the only recent immigrant applying. With the great influx of immigrants to Canada that is not always the case, but it will at least make you different from the majority of the applicants. Is that your angle? If you can't come up with anything else it is better than nothing. Remember, though, that you will need to convince the prospective employer that you are likely to hang around for a while. A degree of commitment to Canada must be demonstrated. (Except for temporary or vacation work.)

It can be very effective to point out to the employer how your UK or other experience can be put to good use in the new job. You may, for example, be trained in an area in which the British have always been admired. The service industries, education and training, nursing and engineering all fall into this category. Make a special point of this when submitting your application.

Or perhaps your prospective employer is specifically looking for someone who is dynamic and forward thinking. It wouldn't take much to convince a recruiter that someone who has left their homeland to live many miles away in another country is pretty dynamic and not afraid to take chances!

### Doing your research

Time spent on research is never wasted and can often mean the difference between landing the job or not. Your local library is a goldmine of information. If the company you are applying to is fairly large you will be able to find its annual report there. Also, check the periodical indexes for articles about that company. Other useful research tools include:

- *Canadian Key Business Directory*
- *Financial Post 100 Best Companies to Work for*
- *Directory of Associations in Canada*
- *CANTECH National Directory*
- *Classified Directory: A Complete Guide to Business in Canada*
- *Directory of Canadian Manufacturers*
- *Co-op Program Directory*
- *Magazines Career Directory.*

## PERFECTING THE RESUME

In the previous chapter we looked at the differences between an English-style CV and the North American-style résumé. We also stressed the importance of tailoring your résumé to the specific job applied for. This can often simply be a question of emphasis. You can't change your experience and education but you *can* highlight the areas that make you ideal for that particular job.

### Making your résumé fit the job

Figures 17, 18 and 19 show an example of this tailoring. Figure 17 is a 'generic' résumé. From it you will see that Jean Marchand has a fairly wide range of administrative experience, from insurance work to public relations to fund raising. Figure 18 is the newspaper advertisement for the job she is interested in. Note that Jean has some of the experience required but fails to meet the specification of familiarity with the local area. Her relevant experience with non-profit organisations comprises only a very small part of her career to date.

Figure 19 shows how she tweaked her résumé to highlight her suitability for this particular position and minimise the areas in which she could be seen to fall short. There wasn't a great deal Jean could do about the lack of local area knowledge, she will have to hope her other qualifications outweigh that disadvantage. As the advertisement didn't mention any requirements for administrative/secretarial experience, that aspect of her career was played down in favour of highlighting the experience at the women's centre. Even that has been modified to emphasise those elements mentioned in the advertisement: fund raising and volunteer supervision. A couple of points have been added under Additional Information that are relevant to the sort of job advertised. Jean's cover letter will do even more to bring her relevant experience to the recruiter's attention.

Résumé of
Jean Marchand

1881 Arbutus St
Vancouver
BC V6V 1L2
tel 604 887 8865
fax 604 887 8754

**JOB OBJECTIVE:** Administration, Public Relations and Publishing

**EMPLOYMENT**

1992–1996    Editorial Assistant, *Food Science* magazine, Oxford
Publishing, Oxford, UK.
Responsible for the administration of a monthly scientific
journal. Maintaining, modifying and administering four
databases containing information relating to articles and
authors. Daily contact with authors and referees in order to
achieve swift and smooth copy flow.

1990–1992    Coordinator, Southampton Women's Drop-In Centre,
Southampton, UK.
Complete responsibility for administration of this
government-funded society. Coordinated a 24-hour-a-day
crisis phone-line in conjunction with local police. Arranged
and presented lectures and courses in the community.
Handled all radio, newspaper and local television interviews
and articles. Supervised volunteers and participated in fund
raising.

1986–1990    Secretary/Office Manager/Agent, Winsome Insurance
Agency, Southampton, UK.
Responsible for all administrative aspects of running a small
insurance agency, including assessing and issuing policies,
as well as advising clients in my capacity of licensed
insurance agent.

**EDUCATION**

1989    Hatfield Polytechnic, Hatfield, UK
Other Than Life Insurance Agents Licence

1982–1989    Hammersmith Secondary, London, UK
General Certificate of Education A-Levels (equivalent to post
high school diploma) in English, History, Business Studies
and Art.

**ADDITIONAL INFORMATION**

Typing speed: 60 words per minute
Audio typing and shorthand experience
Driving licence (UK)
Computer literate with experience of WP 5.1, Filemaker Pro,
Lotus 123, Harvard Graphics

References available on request.

Fig. 17. Generic résumé.

116

**JOB ADVERTISEMENT FROM THE *VANCOUVER SUN***

**Fund Raiser**
**Event Co-ordinator – Surrey**

Training and/or experience in non-profit organizations specifically: (1) fund raising, including gaming (2) Coordinating fund raising events & (3) supervising volunteers & familiarity with the Surrey area. Position duration 1 year with possible renewal. Fax complete résumé detailing requested background and salary expectations to: 588-1234 by January 29.

Fig. 18. Specific job advertisement.

## WRITING THE PERFECT COVERING LETTER

It is debatable which is more important – the résumé or the covering letter. Certainly it is in the covering letter that your personality can show through, as well as your enthusiasm. This is where you sell yourself.

### Making the right connections

Think about what you are trying to get across to the recruiter. Your aim should be to convince her/him that it is worth having a closer look at your résumé. More than that, you want the recruiter to decide that you are worth interviewing, that you have something tangible to offer that company. The most effective way of achieving this is to make favourable comparisons wherever possible.

- Connect your career goals and past experience to the requirements of this position.

- Connect your special areas of expertise to the job specification.

- Connect your interests to the area in which the prospective employer operates. Make it obvious that you are absolutely right for the job.

Be certain that you provide all the information asked for in the job advertisement. In the example above the employer requested salary expectations, so your covering letter should contain that information.

Résumé of
Jean Marchand

1881 Arbutus St
Vancouver
BC V6V 1L2
tel 604 887 8865
fax 604 887 8754

**JOB OBJECTIVE:** Event Coordinator/Fund Raiser

**EMPLOYMENT**

1992–1996     Editorial Assistant, *Food Science* magazine, Oxford
Publishing, Oxford, UK.
Responsible for the administration of a monthly scientific
journal. Database administration and management. Daily
contact with authors. Supervision of part-time clerical help.

1990–1992     Coordinator, Southampton Women's Drop-In Centre,
Southampton, UK.
Complete responsibility for administration of this
government-funded society. Coordinated various fund raising
events including successful dinners, entertainment evenings
and raffles. Arranged and presented lectures and courses in
the community and approached local companies with
requests for funding assistance. Liaison with local media
including radio and television interviews and press releases.
Coordinated volunteer recruitment and supervised activities
for volunteers.

1986–1990     Secretary/Office Manager/Agent, Winsome Insurance
Agency, Southampton, UK.
Responsible for all administrative aspects of running a small
insurance agency. Advising clients in my capacity of
licensed insurance agent. Supervision of clerical help.

**EDUCATION**

1989     Hatfield Polytechnic, Hatfield, UK
Other Than Life Insurance Agents Licence

1982–1989     Hammersmith Secondary, London, UK
General Certificate of Education A-Levels (equivalent to post
high school diploma) in English, History, Business Studies
and Art.

**ADDITIONAL INFORMATION**

Typing speed: 60 words per minute
Audio typing and shorthand experience
Driving licence (UK)
Computer literate with experience of WP 5.1, Filemaker Pro,
Lotus 123, Harvard Graphics
Past President of Kidlington Amateur Dramatic Society
Volunteer Campaigner for Heart Foundation

Fig. 19. Tailored résumé.

## Essential elements

Each application is different and you will have to gear your letter to the tone and content of the job advertisement. However, there are several elements that ought to be in every cover letter you send:

- Address the letter to a person, not a position or, even worse, the dreaded Dear Sirs. If a name is not stated in the advertisement, or you are writing on spec, give the company a call and ask for the name of the personnel manager.

- Always name the position you are applying for. Personalise your letter wherever possible. Nobody likes to receive a form letter.

- Mention any documents you are enclosing with your application such as résumé, references. This demonstrates an organised approach as well as drawing them to the recruiter's attention.

- Be as specific as possible when outlining your suitability. It is better to say that you have experience of several named software programmes than make the blanket statement that you are computer literate.

- Say why you want the job and why you think you could do it well. Don't leave it up to the reader to make that connection – they may not!

- Indicate interest in the company and the area in which they work.

- Conclude your letter optimistically. 'I look forward to hearing from you soon' or 'I would be pleased to attend for an interview at a mutually convenient time'. This rounds off your communication in a confident and pleasant manner.

Taking those factors into consideration, how would our hopeful Event Coordinator word her letter?

- There is no name or telephone number given in the job advertisement. It would be worth Jean's while to send a fax stating that she is interested in the position and asking if there is anyone in particular to whom she should address her reply.

- Jean knows the title of the job she is applying for, so she should include this in her opening sentence.

1881 Arbutus St
Vancouver
BC V6V 1L2
tel 604 887 8865
fax 604 887 8754

11 January 199X

Helen Ruffel
Surrey Community Centre
1435 East Road
Surrey
BC V5B 6J2

**FAX: 588 8697**

Dear Ms Ruffel

I am writing to apply for the position of Fund Raiser/Event Coordinator, as advertised in the Vancouver Sun. This is an exciting opportunity and one which I would be very pleased to be considered for. As you will see from the enclosed résumé, I have had considerable experience of fund raising and working with volunteers, as Coordinator of the Southampton Women's Centre. I note that your advertisement specifies experience of fund raising by gaming. One of the most successful fund raising campaigns we ran at the Women's Centre was a monthly bingo evening. Additionally, I have coordinated raffles, tombolas and similar events.

I have taken this opportunity to include some written references that I think you will find relevant to this position, including several personal references from some of the volunteers I recruited and worked with.

I'm sure you will not fail to notice that my career to date has been in the UK. I recently obtained Landed Immigrant Status and arrived in Vancouver two weeks ago. I have to admit it is a city I have fallen in love with and I look forward to making my home here. It would be wonderful if my career could move back into the field of charity organisations, as my work in this area was most enjoyable and rewarding.

With regard to salary expectations, I am looking for appointments in the region of $28,000 to $35,000.

I look forward to hearing from you and would be pleased to meet at any convenient time to discuss the position further.

Yours sincerely

Jean Marchand

encs

Fig. 20. Sample cover letter.

- Jean has some references that are particularly relevant to this position and so has decided to include them in her application. These, and the enclosed résumé, should be mentioned in her letter.

- She has experience in most of the areas specified in the advertisement. She should draw the recruiter's attention to this and stress the similarity between what she did at the women's centre and the requirements of the advertised position.

- Jean should stress how much she enjoyed her work for the charity organisation in Southampton and why she would like to work in this sort of environment again.

- The advertisement asked for details of salary expectations, so this must be included in Jean's letter. That can be an awkward area, as whilst you don't want to blow your chances completely by expecting more than they are willing to pay, you don't want to undervalue your skills or leave yourself open to a low offer. The best way around this is to give a fairly wide range that starts just a bit above the minimum you are willing to accept and goes up to the highest you could reasonably hope for, based on your experience and any knowledge you have of the industry norms. Refer again to the International Pay and Benefits Survey. Many job advertisements do give salaries, so make a note of those for which you are qualified. This will give you a good idea of what you should be aiming for.

Jean's covering letter (or in this case covering fax) is shown in Figure 20.

## MAXIMISING YOUR ASSETS

As the song says, 'Accentuate the positive, eliminate the negative'. This advice is applicable throughout the job hunting process, from initial contact to final interview. What are your assets?

- spirit of adventure
- eager for new experience
- adaptability
- ability to organise
- not afraid of big challenges.

Surely all of these are applicable to anyone intrepid enough to consider working in a new country. So point them out.

## Thinking about your personal assets

You will have your own special assets to add to this list. In fact making a list is a good idea. Decide what aspects of your character and experience show you in the best light and figure out ways to bring them into every letter, every résumé you send out, every conversation with a prospective employer. Don't be afraid of repeating yourself. The Canadian employer is used to this sort of approach and is more likely to think that the self-effacing candidate has something to hide than to applaud his reticence.

Flexibility is very important in the Canadian job market. Jobs tend to be somewhat less structured than you may be used to and you could well be expected to 'muck in' as the occasion demands, particularly in a smaller firm. Once again, someone making the move to a different country is nothing if not flexible. Remind the prospective employer of that.

## Eliminating the negative

Whilst you must be seen to be keen on your new country, you should avoid any negative references to the old one or your job experiences there. Indeed, avoid all negative references completely. Concentrate on the positive aspects of your move, how your different experience could give an employer a vital edge and how keen you are to put all the knowledge that you have gained to work for them.

## MAKING YOURSELF MEMORABLE

A technique used in sales is to focus on some unique aspect of your character or appearance and mention that repeatedly. The idea is that the customer (in your case the prospective employer) will remember you when making a decision regarding his purchase (appointment). That is not so easy when your first communications are all written, but it can be done. Again, you have the advantage of being distinctive as a foreigner. You can use that to make the recruiter remember you. You will, of course, have mentioned your Landed Immigrant Status or Employment Authorisation in your cover letter (not least to reassure the recruiter that you can legally work in Canada). When you come to chase up the application with a phone call your accent will make you recognisable. It gives you a talking point, too.

## Phoning the company

Follow-up phone calls in themselves are a way of getting yourself noticed. In most cases it is perfectly acceptable to give the company a call if you have not had any response to your application after a week or so. Beware, however, of the advertisement which specifically requests that you do not phone. These are becoming more frequent.

On the other hand, sometimes an advertisement will invite applicants to phone for further information or 'an informal chat'. Don't waste these opportunities to make yourself memorable. It is not possible to overstate the value of that British accent (assuming that is what you have!). It will nearly always be an immediate point in your favour.

### Sending photos and references

An increasingly common practice is the inclusion of a photograph with your application. This is not the norm in Canada, nor is it unacceptable. Use your judgement. If you think there is something about your appearance that will emphasise your suitability for the job, enclose a photo. Many employers in service industries have a strong interest in what candidates look like and only consider those of an appropriate appearance.

If you have written references that relate very well to the job you are applying for, enclose copies of these at the initial application stage. Another way of getting yourself remembered.

### CHECKLIST

- Identify an angle, something that makes you stand out from the crowd.

- Spend some time on your résumé. Tailor it to the specifications of each job you apply for. Highlight experience which illustrates your suitability for that position.

- Your cover letter is very important, it is here that you really sell yourself. Point out the experience and qualifications that make you ideal for the job. Adopt a confident approach.

- Make connections between your past experience and the requirements for this job. Point them out in your cover letter.

- Whenever possible make telephone contact with potential employers. Be careful not to do this, however, when job advertisements specifically instruct you not to phone.

- 'Accentuate the positive, eliminate the negative.'

## CASE STUDIES

### Samantha makes her mark

Sam has now been in Vancouver for a month and has settled in well to her new job and new way of life. Not for her the uncertainty of applying for jobs; she is lucky to have found one before she left England. However, one day she looks on the staff notice board and learns that a position senior to hers has just become vacant. She decides to apply for it.

Samantha has a look at her CV and realises that it does not conform to the résumé style expected in Canada. It also does not mention her recent experience. She asks to use a friend's word processor and turns her CV into a résumé.

'That notice specified they wanted someone "not afraid of a challenge",' her friend observes. 'That certainly applies to you!'

'Why do you say that?'

'Well, you have just crossed the Atlantic and one entire continent to start work in a new country. You should point that out in your letter.'

Samantha refers to her move as a challenge in her covering letter. She is delighted when, one week later, she is called to interview.

### George makes the change

George is nervous of his decision to try for a bit of a career move. He has not worked in a recording studio before.

'But you did do that volunteer work in the hospital sorting out their broadcast equipment,' his wife reminds him.

'And I did an extra year's training in audio electronics.'

George needs to highlight this experience in his 'tweaked' résumé. This will draw attention to his suitability for work in a recording studio, rather than emphasise any lack of experience.

### Lucy gets restless

Although grateful for the job waiting for her at the Burger Bar, Lucy is keen to see more of Canada. Metropolitan Montreal doesn't really suit her – she still longs for those wide open spaces!

She has seen an advertisement for clerical help in a provincial forest fire-fighting department. The ad invites applicants to phone for an informal chat.

Lucy calls and has an in-depth conversation with the recruiter, who is very impressed by her enthusiasm. Lucy asks lots of questions about the trees and conservation techniques. The recruiter makes a note to place Lucy on the short-list for interview.

## DISCUSSION POINTS

1. List your experience, qualifications and qualities that would make a prospective employer want to hire you. Put them in order of importance. How can you put these qualities across in an initial contact letter? What about in person?

2. What things have you done in the past, either at work or in leisure time, that illustrate your positive assets?

3. How can you make yourself memorable? Is there anything you can put in a cover letter that would achieve this? How about later, at the interview stage?

4. Would it be advantageous to enclose a photograph with your application?

# 8
# Landing Your Job

## PREPARING FOR INTERVIEW

### Doing some research

Probably the most useful thing you can do to prepare for your interview is a bit of research about the firm. This needn't be exhaustive but could include finding out about the company's products and any competition. Anyone intending to get ahead in the Canadian workplace is expected to be an enthusiastic go-getter.

You should go armed with a knowledge of the pay scales in your field. That will not be difficult, as Canadian employers and employees tend to be pretty open about salaries and these are usually mentioned in job advertisements.

### Your appearance

Generally you should dress less formally than you would for an interview in the UK, although it depends on the type of position for which you are applying. Whereas in the UK a prospective employer will expect an interviewee to arrive in a suit or equivalent, the Canadian employer could be rather intimidated if you were to turn up in your best bib and tucker for a job in, say, a production environment. Choose an outfit that is just slightly more formal than you would expect to wear in your new job on a daily basis.

### What to take with you

You may not need all the following, but best to be on the safe side:

- Social Insurance Card. Your prospective employer may want to ensure that you have completed all the formalities necessary for starting work in Canada.

- Passport. Again the employer may wish to confirm that you are qualified to work in Canada. If applicable, the Landed Immigrant Status document stapled into the back of your passport will reassure him.

- References. Although you will have sent relevant references with your application it is a good idea to take the originals with you. The employer is not likely to want to telephone the UK to confirm your credentials so the more written documentation you can give him the better. Take along also any character references you obtained before leaving the UK. It all helps. Figure 21 is a sample of a character reference.

- Copy of the job advertisement. Useful to refer to.

- Another copy of your resumé, again for you to refer to.

---

George Sanders
136 West Street
Luton UK LU6 123

3 November 199X

TO WHOM IT MAY CONCERN

I have been asked to supply a character reference for Alan Morton, who has been an enthusiastic and valued member of our amateur dramatics club for the past three years. I was, of course, sorry to learn that Alan would be leaving us, but feel sure that he will do well in his new venture. To be honest, I was not surprised to learn that he was planning to move to a new country, as Alan seems to thrive on challenges and I have always found I could rely on him to come up with innovative solutions to all manner of problems.

Alan has been a real asset to our club over the years and leaves behind many friends.

Yours faithfully

George Sanders
Chairman, Luton Amateur Dramatic Society (LADS)

---

Fig. 21. Sample character reference letter.

## Being punctual

This next piece of advice may seem odd, but it is a fact. Canadians are discomfited if you arrive early for your interview. I don't know why but I have seen it several times. It embarrasses them to have you turn up more than five minutes before your appointment. So take a turn around the block if necessary and report for interview at precisely the arranged time.

## PRESENTING YOURSELF WELL AT THE INTERVIEW

The following list of ten interview tips was prepared and issued by the Canada Employment Centre, so we must assume that it will lead you to the sort of interview behaviour favoured by the Canadian employer.

### Ten interview tips

1. Dress neatly and appropriately. Do they wear suits, or dress casually?

2. Map your route in advance so that you arrive in good time.

3. Don't smoke or chew gum.

4. Greet the interviewer with a handshake.

5. Don't sit until the interviewer sits or asks you to.

6. Be calm, poised and efficient.

7. Answer questions honestly and concisely.

8. Show enthusiasm and interest.

9. Bring copies of your résumé, letters of reference or certificates that are relevant.

10. Focus on a specific job or jobs. From an employer's point of view an applicant eager to accept 'anything' may do nothing well.

Some of those are pretty obvious but they will give you an idea of the Canadian attitude.

### The information interview

There is another sort of interview: the purpose of an information interview is to have an informal talk with someone who works in the field which interests you. You attend simply to gather information and neither party feels pressured into either asking for a job or offering one. But it can lead to openings and will provide you with the names of the people in a position to hire, as well as some inside knowledge of that particular company or field.

You must not, in these circumstances, present yourself as looking for a job. You want to find out:

• how the organisation works

• what jobs may be suitable for you

• what additional skills you may need

• how to get to talk to the person who does the hiring.

## ACCENTUATING THE POSITIVE

One of the first questions the interviewer is likely to ask is why you have moved to Canada. Make sure that your reply is positive. Don't say derogatory things about the UK or your life there as that will only establish you as a moaner. Point out instead the opportunities that are available in Canada and your own goals for improvement. Show yourself to be a go-getter. Be careful, though, not to give the impression that you are likely to flit off to pastures greener. Indicate commitment to your new life in Canada. Most Canadians are proud of their country and will be pleased that you wish to be a part of it.

The prospective employer may feel that your lack of working experience in Canada could be a disadvantage. Turn this around by pointing out that you can bring a fresh outlook and new ways of looking at things. Canadians are not averse to change for the better! Remember that most Canadians (the Anglophone ones, anyway) are attracted to things British. If you are going to be working with the public this could be a distinct advantage.

### Showing you are adaptable

Draw attention to your adaptability. It is a valued trait in the Canadian job market. Many companies are small (less than 50 people) and job descriptions tend to be much less structured than you may be used to. It is often the case of everybody 'mucking in' to get the job done or the product out. This is true even in larger companies, many of which down-sized during the recession and now do not have sufficient personnel to deal with the recent rapid recovery of the economy.

**National**

New Year's Day
Good Friday
Easter Monday
Victoria Day                  Monday before 25 May
Canada Day                1 July*
Labour Day               first Monday in September
Thanksgiving            second Monday in October
Remembrance Day      11 November
Christmas Day
Boxing Day

**Provincial**

Alberta
    Family Day               third Monday in February
    Heritage Day            first Monday in August

British Columbia
    BC Day                 first Monday in August

Manitoba
    Civic holiday            usually first Monday in August

Newfoundland (holidays are usually observed on nearest Monday)
    Commonwealth Day    second Monday in March
    St Patrick's Day        17 March
    St George's Day       23 April
    Discovery Day         27 June
    Memorial Day         7 July
    Orangemen's Day     10 July

Ontario
    Civic holiday            usually first Monday in August

Quebec
    Quebec Day          24 June

Saskatchewan
    Civic holiday            first Monday in August

Yukon
    Discovery Day         third Monday in August

Northwest Territories
    Civic holiday            usually first Monday in August

*(or 2 July where 1 July is a Sunday)

Fig. 22. Canadian public statutory holidays.

## NEGOTIATING TERMS

### Leave
Some things such as holiday and sick leave are usually pretty inflexible, and, in general, less generous than those in the UK. Expect only about ten days' allowance for sick leave and, usually, two weeks' holiday leave (known as vacation). The latter may improve after you have been some time with the company.

There are several public holidays each year and you will be entitled to these (or time off in lieu). There are two types of public holiday: the federal days apply across the whole country while each province also has its own holidays. These are outlined in Figure 22.

### Hours
A 35 to 40-hour working week is the norm, although this is becoming less common. Many Canadians work at one or more part-time jobs. Statistics Canada recently issued a report showing that the number of people working part-time has doubled since 1975 from 20 per cent to 39 per cent. One quarter of all jobs in Canada in 1994 were part-time.

You may well find yourself working considerably longer hours than those stated in your contract. This is largely due to under-staffing. You will be expected to cooperate and should eventually be rewarded with advancement within the company. This does not, of course, apply to jobs with hourly rates where overtime is paid.

Flexi-time is common, with core working hours of 10am to 4pm, but you will be expected to make up time for doctor and dentist appointments.

### Pay
This is where your earlier research comes in. A small company will be more flexible on the subject of salary, whereas larger companies usually have fixed salary bands.

### Working conditions
There is no overall federal policy on pay and working conditions, although each province has its own regulations. If you have any concerns contact the Employment Division in the province you have moved to, or ask the Canada Employment Centre to advise you.

### Trades unions
Trades unions are active in many segments of Canadian industry. Approximately one-third of Canada's labour force belong to a trade

union. See Useful Addresses for the major organisations with which almost all Canadian trades unions are affiliated.

**Other things to ask about**
There are various perks and incentives throughout the industries. Establish if any of these are offered:

• As outlined earlier, provincial health insurance schemes (Medicare) are available and very good value for money. Some employers will make your contributions, so ask about this.

• Dental plan. Dental treatment is not included under Medicare, but many firms have group policies.

• Pensions and life assurance. These benefits follow much the same pattern as in UK companies.

• Bonuses. As in the UK many firms offer incentive and profit-share schemes.

• Overtime. Enquire as to individual company policy.

**STARTING YOUR NEW JOB**

**The first day**
Bring with you:

• National Insurance card
• Medical card (if your employer is going to make your contributions).

As far as dress code is concerned, follow more or less the same rules as for the interview. Be led by what you observed co-workers wearing. It is probably inevitable that you will have a tendency at first to overdress. Don't worry – they will probably see it as a charming example of English eccentricity!

**Fitting in**
You may find the Canadian attitude to time-keeping more laid back than you are used to. But remember that works both ways. If additional hours are required from you it is expected that you will oblige willingly and cheerfully.
  A fairly informal atmosphere is likely to prevail, especially in smaller

companies. Follow the lead of your co-workers when deciding whether to address superiors by their first names. You will be on first-name terms with your work mates and probably your immediate superior. It is almost a prerequisite of work in a Canadian company that you be willing to socialise outside working hours. Many companies arrange outings, sporting events and family days. You could be considered snobbish or unfriendly if you do not join in.

**A reminder about tax**
Although Canadian employers deduct tax from your income at source, you will be required to complete your own return at the end of the tax year (April). So if you incur tax-deductible expenses during the course of your job make notes and keep receipts from the beginning.

**CHECKLIST**

• Find out something about the business of the company to which you are applying.

• Arm yourself with a good idea of salary expectations.

• Take your Social Insurance card, passport and all references.

• Be positive. Show your enthusiasm and adaptability.

• Find out about benefits and incentives.

• Don't be too formal. Take your lead from co-workers in matters of dress and etiquette.

**QUESTIONS AND ANSWERS**

Now that you have that all-important interview lined up, time spent in preparation can make all the difference.

1. *What makes you right for this job?*

How can you draw on past experience to demonstrate your suitability for this particular position?

Have you worked in a similar field or undertaken other tasks of this nature?

What do you know about this sphere of business?

Do you have any ideas on how this firm could increase their performance/profitability?

## POSSIBLE PITFALLS AND HOW TO AVOID THEM
### You are asked why you left your home to work in Canada

*Negative response*
You talk about the boring life you had and how much you disliked working conditions in the UK.

*Positive response*
You explain that, although happy in your work, you felt the need of new horizons and fresh challenges.

*Outcome*
Your prospective employer perceives you as a malcontent and fears you will always be complaining.

*Outcome*
The interviewer regards you as an ambitious and forward thinking person who is adaptable and eager.

### The interviewer addresses you by your first name and adopts a very informal attitude

*Negative response*
You are unused to this degree of informality and continue to call the interviewer 'Mr Smith', although this obviously makes him uncomfortable.

*Positive response*
Although you initially respond formally you soon realise that the interviewer prefers a more relaxed atmosphere, so you switch to the friendlier approach.

*Outcome*
You are seen as being rather too straight-laced for this company, which prides itself on its friendly atmosphere.

*Outcome*
You are seen as a friendly and outgoing type who will fit in well with this company.

### You are interviewed by a small firm for a newly created position with no specific job description

*Negative response*
You stress the need for comprehensive job descriptions and a strict definition of roles.

*Positive response*
You show that you understand the need for flexibility in smaller companies and offer suggestions as to how the position might evolve.

*Outcome*
You are not offered the job as it is feared that you will not meet the varying demands of an up-and-coming company.

*Outcome*
The interviewer is impressed by your understanding of working conditions in small firms and keen to hear more of your ideas for development.

2. *How does your international background make you a better candidate?*

The interviewer wants to be sure that you are committed to your new life. How can you convince him/her that you really intend to make a mark in Canada?

> What are your real reasons for deciding to work in Canada?
> Will these be acceptable to a prospective employer?
> What differences can you see between working practices in Canada and the UK?
> How would this knowledge be valuable to a prospective employer?

3. *Can you fit in to the Canadian workplace?*

Do you have an open attitude towards working hours?

> Are you willing to put in extra time when required?
> Are you prepared to cope with a less formal structure at work?
> Does this make you uncomfortable in any way?
> What are your feelings regarding socialising with colleagues outside of working hours?
> Would you regard this as an imposition?

4. *What makes you memorable?*

Someone who has decided to live and work in another country already stands out from the crowd. What can you say at the interview that will emphasise this and draw attention to your adaptability?

> Have you considered what the average Canadian's perception is of people of your nationality?
> How can you utilise this to your advantage?
> Are you willing to 'play' on your differences, should that seem appropriate?

## CASE STUDIES

### Samantha turns a deficit into an asset

Samantha attends an interview for the position of senior dietitian. She has not met the interviewer before. He expresses concern that she might find working practices rather different from those she has been used to in England. As she will need to deal with both patients and management in the new position, he fears this may be a problem.

'I can see that the set-up here is different, and after being here for a while I think I've got quite a good handle on it,' Sam replies. 'But I regard that as a challenge rather than a drawback. As you can see from these references I have worked in a variety of health care situations and I feel that adaptability is one of my strong points.'

When asked about her long-term plans, Sam does not mention that she intends to return to England in a few years' time, but instead enthuses about the lifestyle in Vancouver and how well she feels it suits her.

The interviewer, who is already impressed with her credentials, feels that Sam has the right attitude to adapt to different working practices and offers her the position.

## George does his research
George Robins is asked to come for an interview at Eastern Audio, a small recording studio which supplements its trade by bulk cassette duplicating. George studies the market carefully before his appointment and when asked what he feels he could contribute to the company is able to offer an informed reply.

'From what I understand, Eastern Audio doesn't have a lot of competition locally so there is ample opportunity for expansion. However, a major concern must be the falling market in cassettes, due to the growth of the CD market. I have some ideas as to how to tap into that market and have some design ideas that may interest you.'

George goes on to explain that he would be happy to put in extra time to develop those ideas and adds that he has already discussed this with his wife, who is supportive.

Eastern Audio's engineering manager is impressed with George's enthusiasm and commitment and feels he would make a useful addition to the team.

## Lucy gives the wrong impression
In a heavily forested area an entire department of the provincial government is devoted solely to preventing and containing forest fires. Lucy is delighted to be asked to come and speak to the personnel manager about a clerical opening in this department. After describing the position the interviewer asks Lucy why she left Britain.

'It's really dreadful there. I must have applied for a hundred jobs after I left school. But no luck. I went to quite a few interviews but nothing came of any of them. And the jobs were so dull, anyway.'

The interview does not last much longer. The personnel manager wonders why Lucy failed to get a job despite going to so many interviews and is concerned that she may be a moaner who would not be willing to undertake mundane tasks.

## DISCUSSION POINTS

1. Gather together your written references. Which ones illustrate your enthusiasm and adaptability? How can you draw the interviewer's attention to these?

2. Make a list of all the possible benefits available. Which would be particularly valuable to you? Could any be used as bargaining tools in negotiation?

3. Imagine what questions the interviewer is likely to ask you. How can you formulate your answers to demonstrate a positive attitude?

# 9
# Moving Onwards and Upwards

## RECOGNISING OPPORTUNITIES

The first job you take in Canada may not be exactly what you are
looking for. It's not unlike the situation when you first joined the work
force after leaving school: you need to get your foot on the ladder. The
newspaper *Canada News* recently reported that trained professionals
who immigrated to Canada were finding it difficult to compete with
their Canadian counterparts, even if the immigrants' qualifications and
experience were superior. A sobering thought, but not necessarily
daunting: it simply becomes necessary to adopt a career strategy. You
may need to accept a position lower on the professional ladder than
you currently hold, but the tradition of advancement is a strong one in
the Canadian workplace. Look out for the opportunities and you can
soon regain your status and begin to improve on it.

### Gaining advancement
The most obvious means of advancement is from within the company
you are working for. That is dealt with a bit later in this chapter.
Canada's economy is strong and growing and once you have made your
mark your opportunities need not be limited. Keep your finger on the
pulse of what is happening within your field of expertise. Keep up with
Canadian politics and watch the economy. You may see a chance to
make a lateral move within your field. And don't forget to keep an eye
on all regions of Canada. There is a great deal going on and new
opportunities arise all the time.

## WEIGHING THE OPTIONS

If the chance of advancement within your company does not look
promising you might consider these options.

### Changing locale
Canada is a changing, growing country and opportunities you might

not have previously considered can present themselves. For example, Vancouver is swiftly becoming the Hollywood of the North, with major motion pictures filmed there in whole or in part, as well as TV programmes such as *The X-Files*. Is that something you might be able to take advantage of?

## Upgrading your qualifications

Perhaps even more so than in Britain, Canadian employers are impressed by anyone keen to improve their qualifications and employability. Many Canadians regularly attend night school to enhance their job prospects. Courses are extremely varied and widely available. Look in your regional newspapers and *Yellow Pages*. The following federal government agencies dealing with occupational training may also be of help:

Employment and Immigration Canada
Public Inquiries Centre
Public Affairs Branch
140 Promenade du Portage
Phase IV
Hull
PQ K1A 0J9.
Tel: (819) 994 6313. Fax: (819) 994 0116.

Public Service Commission
Training Programs Branch
Ottawa
ON K1A 0M7.
Tel: (613) 991 4636. Fax: (613) 999 7859.

Refer also to Useful Addresses for departments dealing with provincial occupational training.

## Self-employment

It is not necessarily true that all the world loves an entrepreneur, but certainly the Canadian provincial and federal governments seem to. Both are placing a great emphasis on job creation, and offer assistance and incentives to those wishing to start up a business that will create employment for other Canadians. Municipal governments can also provide guidance. Look in your local *Yellow Pages* under Government for further information.

The Canadian Employment Centre national office recently issued a list of business opportunities that are projected to do well through the rest of the 1990s and beyond:

- health care/home care services
- retirement homes located in attractive small towns
- auto services, repair/maintenance work done in customers' driveways
- entertainment programming for the expanded cable networks
- software, software, software
- personal and home security systems
- custom clothing, including shoes especially for seniors
- foreign language training
- home office products and services
- environmental products to protect drinking water and assist with waste disposal
- low fat/low sodium foods and meats
- inexpensive fast food
- audio and visual aids for older individuals
- special travel opportunities for older travellers
- healthy, natural pesticide-free foods
- interactive technology, cellular phones and home theatre equipment.

You might also like to take a look at *Entrepreneur Magazine's The Complete Guide to Owning a Home-Based Business.*

## Other foreign opportunities
If you still have the globe-trotting urge keep up your contacts with the ex-pat network by subscribing to publications such as *Overseas Jobs Express* and *The Expatriate*. Often employers will favour a proven ex-pat who can demonstrate flexibility and the ability to adapt to new conditions.

## Unemployment benefits
There is a qualifying period for the federal unemployment insurance scheme so it will only apply if you have been in work for about six months. Should you find yourself unemployed after a period of work in Canada head to the CEC and sign on for UIC. UIC stands for Unemployment Insurance Commission, which is the government body administering the system, but the benefits themselves are also referred to as UIC.

## RISING WITHIN THE COMPANY

The potential for upward movement in the Canadian workplace is good. Show yourself to be a go-getter. Identify areas where expansion is possible and let it be known that you would like to be a part of that growth.

### Establishing your reputation

If your company is large enough to have a personnel or human resources department make certain that the officers are informed of your career goals. In a smaller company you should make your immediate superior and possibly his boss aware of your aims. If you are willing to relocate be sure to let them know. If you are interested in training for new areas within the company they should be aware of this also. It will do you no harm to get a reputation as someone who is keen to advance and willing to accommodate change.

If you do take any courses to improve your position, inform your employer. Try to make it plain how your increased knowledge would be of use to their company.

Research can be a valuable tool. Find out all you can about the company you are working for and the marketplace. If you can identify an area for expansion let your employer know how you could play a part. Even if that falls through you will be seen as dynamic.

You may be well placed for any relocations available within your company as you have already demonstrated that you are able to make a major move and adapt to new conditions. If any such positions arise, emphasise your experience.

## UTILISING YOUR EXPERIENCE

If you had to take a step down the corporate or professional ladder, perhaps because your professional qualifications did not translate well into the Canadian market, don't let it stop you. Contact The Canadian Information Centre for International Credentials to find out what you need to do to gain the necessary accreditation. Often it will only be a matter of taking an examination or doing a short course. Sometimes you will need to have a certain amount of Canadian experience.

Searching for a job in a new country can be a daunting experience, but you have done it successfully. In the course of your search you will have identified many sources of information and channels through which to find a job. Should you decide on a change, take advantage of the knowledge you have gained and start a campaign on much the same lines.

This time you will have the added advantage of Canadian work experience.

## RETURNING HOME

There are three main reasons why you might leave Canada and return home.

### You have completed a temporary/vacation job or exchange visit

This is pretty straightforward. You will have taken only necessary possessions with you, so it is probably just a case of packing a couple of large suitcases and getting on a prearranged flight. If you have opened any accounts during your stay make sure these are cleared or you have made arrangements for payment. Remember to collect any relevant references from your Canadian employers.

### You were temporarily relocated to Canada by your UK employer

The circumstances are going to vary greatly when a secondment is completed, but in most cases a great deal of the necessary arrangements will be made by your employer. It is up to you, however, to clear up all personal details such as credit payments.

### Personal reasons necessitate a return

There could be many different reasons why you feel you have to leave Canada, from having to return home to care for an elderly parent to having tried it and not liked it. If the latter is the case it is important that you adopt a good attitude toward the situation, not look on the venture as a failure. You made the move, you got a job in a foreign country and made a home there. Now you have surveyed your situation and decided that you prefer your home country. That is perfectly acceptable.

It is going to be almost as complex and exhausting moving back home as it was leaving in the first place. You do not have to worry about work permits, immigration status or learning about the country, but you will need to make all the same arrangements regarding paying off creditors, dealing with income tax, selling your house and car, engaging movers. There is the question of a job back home. Do the same as you did when you started your venture and begin your job search before you leave. First step might be to contact your last UK employer. Get relatives and friends to send you the jobs section of various British newspapers. Start contacting international and UK recruitment agencies.

## Landed Immigrant Status

A word of warning. Your Landed Immigrant Status becomes invalid if you make your home outside Canada for any great length of time. This is referred to as abandoning Canada as your place of residence, and defined as having frequent and/or lengthy absences from Canada.

## SIGNING OFF

The title of this final chapter could be applied to the whole adventure, from making your decision to work in Canada, achieving the necessary immigration permissions, deciding where to work, finding the right job and settling in.

The preceding pages contain a great deal of information about how to achieve your goal. The rest of the book outlines that information in an easy-to-find format. I hope that it will be helpful and that you enjoy your Canadian experience. The Canadian way of life is both unique and rewarding. Although there may appear to be many similarities between the UK and Canada, at times the differences can seem as vast as the country itself. Even the common language is not always the same. Many everyday items are known by completely different names. For example, a biscuit is a cookie and a cracker is a biscuit! Your car does not have a bonnet and a boot, but a hood and a trunk.

As well as the changes in vocabulary, the Canadian accent can take some getting used to. Although far from universal the rising inflection at the end of sentences and the frequent use of 'eh?' is something you will soon become used to hearing. On that note you may appreciate the following description of how Canada was named.

> Three early settlers – Dave, Bill and George – were sitting around the campfire one evening congratulating themselves on having found such a plentiful and pleasant land. They were, however, concerned that their new home was as yet un-named. Dave suggested that they put letters of the alphabet into a hat and draw them out at random until a suitable name suggested itself. This they did. Digging deep into the hat each of the three settlers drew out a letter. And thus Canada was named.
>
> Dave:      I got a 'C', eh?'
> Bill:       I got an 'N', eh?'
> George:   I got a 'D', eh?'

Good luck, eh!

## CHECKLIST

- Be prepared to take a step down on the career ladder, but be aware of how you can recover that lost ground.

- Find out what you can do to upgrade your qualifications and/or translate them into Canadian equivalents.

- Be on the lookout for advancement within your company. Make sure that your employers are aware of your career goals.

- Consider the option of self-employment.

- Your chances of career advancement could be improved by embarking on further training.

- Keep your finger on what is happening with the Canadian economy. Be on the lookout for opportunities.

- If you decide to return home clear up as many loose ends as possible before you leave. If possible set your job search in motion before leaving Canada.

## CASE STUDIES

### Samantha goes home

Although she thoroughly enjoyed her three years in Canada Sam is now ready to return to England. She is concerned about her mother, who is getting a bit frail and, in any case, she had no intention of making Canada her home for good. She ties up all the loose ends in Canada and heads back to the UK. There she finds some people's attitude difficult.

'So, couldn't hack it, huh?'

'Weren't the streets paved with gold after all?'

'I'm sorry it didn't work out.'

Patiently but firmly, Sam explains that her time in Canada was an adventure and that she thoroughly enjoyed it but felt it was time to return home for many reasons. She emphasises how glad she is to have had the Canadian experience. In so doing she ensures that no one, herself included, perceives her return home as a failure.

## George makes a move

Although George did find a job in a recording studio, it was not really the sort of thing he had in mind, his real aim being to move into the actual recording side of things, rather than technical engineering.

He keeps an eye on all that is happening in the recording industry in Canada, subscribing to several professional publications and keeping his ear to the ground at work. Soon he identifies several opportunities in Vancouver. With the growth of the film industry in that province there are more and more openings for audio experts.

Whilst still retaining his job in Toronto George begins to apply for other studio jobs, and writes several speculative letters to studios in Vancouver. Although he is relatively happy in his job he continues to work towards his final aim.

## Lucy gets the travel bug

Lucy has really enjoyed her time in Canada. She managed to overcome her tendency to moan at interviews and successfully worked her way all across the country. In so doing she caught the travel bug and is now looking at the possibility of doing the same in other countries.

Lucy has contacted several placement agencies which help applicants find work in Australia and New Zealand. Her BUNAC contacts tell her that they, too, operate schemes in those countries. She signs up for one of these and, after five months in Canada, is now off to sample Australia.

## DISCUSSION POINTS

1. You will have become aware of many avenues for job searches. Which of these will remain relevant once you have landed a job? Would it be worthwhile to keep up any subscriptions?

2. How much do you know about the economic growth of Canada? How could you best keep abreast of events that are relevant to your field?

3. Consider the option of further training to improve your chances of promotion. What courses are available to you locally? Do any interest you on a personal as well as a career level? Which would be most impressive to your current or prospective new employer?

4. If you are leaving Canada what references can you gather that will be helpful to you back home?

# Appendix
## Detailed General Occupations List

| CCDO Code | Detailed General Occupations List | Occupation Factor 4 points | SVP Factor 3 points | CCDO Code | Detailed General Occupations List | Occupation Factor 4 points | SVP Factor 3 points |
|---|---|---|---|---|---|---|---|
| 8599-226 | Accordion Repairer | 1 | 15 | 2351-146 | Archivist | 3 | 15 |
| 1171-114 | Accountant | 3 | 18 | 3330-170 | Art director | 3 | 15 |
| 1171-118 | Accountant, budget | 3 | 18 | 3139-115 | Art therapist | 1 | 15 |
| 1171-122 | Accounting, cost | 3 | 18 | 8339-110 | Art-metal worker | 1 | 15 |
| 1171-126 | Accountant, machine processing | 3 | 18 | 3319-122 | Artist, positive | 1 | 11 |
| 1171-130 | Accountant, property | 3 | 18 | 2117-240 | Assayer | 1 | 11 |
| 1171-134 | Accountant, tax | 3 | 18 | 8541-118 | Assembler, frame and mirror | 1 | 11 |
| 2113-110 | Acoustics physicist | 1 | 18 | 2113-114 | Astronomer | 1 | 18 |
| 1176-138 | Acreage-quota-assignment officer | 5 | 11 | 2113-118 | Atomic and molecular physicist | 1 | 18 |
| 2181-118 | Actuary | 1 | 18 | 5149-110 | Auctioneer | 1 | 11 |
| 1179-182 | Administrative officer | 1 | 15 | 2144-126 | Audio engineer | 5 | 18 |
| 3351-162 | Advertising copywriter | 3 | 15 | 3137-110 | Audiologist | 10 | 15 |
| 3315-138 | Aerial photographer | 1 | 15 | 1171-162 | Auditor | 3 | 18 |
| 9111-130 | Aerial survey pilot | 1 | 15 | 2147-122 | Automotive engineer | 5 | 18 |
| 2155-110 | Aerospace eng., design and development | 5 | 18 | 5135-123 | Automotive partsperson | 3 | 11 |
| 2155-126 | Aerospace eng., materials and processes | 5 | 18 | 8581-119 | Automotive techncn, eng & fuel, syst repairs | 1 | 15 |
| 2155-130 | Aerospace engineer, flight operations | 5 | 18 | 8581-120 | Automotive technician, front-end systems | 1 | 15 |
| 2155-134 | Aerospace engineer, flight support | 5 | 18 | 8581-121 | Automotive technician-automatic transmission | 1 | 15 |
| 2155-122 | Aerospace engineer, flight-test | 5 | 18 | 8581-146 | Automotive-air-conditioning mechanic | 1 | 15 |
| 2155-118 | Aerospace engineer, general | 5 | 18 | 8581-166 | Automotive-brake repairer | 1 | 11 |
| 2155-114 | Aerospace engineer, mass properties | 5 | 18 | 8589-114 | Automotive-maintenance-equip servicer | 5 | 15 |
| 2165-210 | Aerospace-engineering technician | 1 | 11 | 8581-170 | Automotive-radiator repairer | 1 | 11 |
| 2165-110 | Aerospace-engineering technologist | 1 | 15 | 3314-130 | Background-and-title artist | 3 | 15 |
| 1179-118 | Agent | 1 | 11 | 2135-240 | Bacteriological technician | 1 | 11 |
| 2111-110 | Agricultural chemist | 1 | 18 | 2135-130 | Bacteriological technologist | 1 | 15 |
| 2311-118 | Agricultural economist | 1 | 18 | 2133-146 | Bacteriologist | 1 | 18 |
| 2159-110 | Agricultural engineer | 5 | 18 | 8213-114 | Baker | 1 | 11 |
| 2131-110 | Agricultural scientist | 1 | 18 | 8584-142 | Bakery-machinery mechanic | 10 | 11 |
| 2135-220 | Agricultural technician | 1 | 11 | 8396-110 | Balancing-machine operator | 1 | 11 |
| 2135-110 | Agricultural technologist | 1 | 15 | 6121-113 | Banquet chef | 10 | 18 |
| 8589-178 | Air-compressor repairer | 5 | 11 | 6143-114 | Barber | 1 | 11 |
| 9113-129 | Air-traffic control assistant | 1 | 11 | 8226-198 | Beer tester | 1 | 11 |
| 9113-120 | Air-traffic control officer | 1 | 15 | 8213-122 | Bench hand | 1 | 11 |
| 9113-118 | Air-traffic controller | 1 | 15 | 2351-122 | Bibliographer | 3 | 15 |
| 3319-113 | Airbrush artist | 1 | 11 | 2133-234 | Biochemist | 1 | 18 |
| 8586-130 | Aircraft engine tester | 3 | 15 | 3156-110 | Biochemistry technologist | 5 | 15 |
| 8586-110 | Aircraft inspector, repair | 3 | 18 | 2135-244 | Biological technician | 1 | 11 |
| 8582-108 | Aircraft maintenance engineer | 1 | 18 | 2135-134 | Biological technologist | 1 | 15 |
| 8582-110 | Aircraft mechanic | 1 | 15 | 2159-123 | Biomedical eng., research & development | 5 | 18 |
| 8399-110 | Aircraft mechanic, experimental | 1 | 18 | 2159-124 | Biomedical engineer, clinical | 5 | 18 |
| 8588-114 | Aircraft-accessories mechanic | 1 | 11 | 8588-115 | Biomedical & laboratory equip repairer | 5 | 15 |
| 8586-134 | Aircraft-hydraulics tester | 3 | 15 | 2133-238 | Biophysicist | 1 | 18 |
| 8588-110 | Aircraft-instrument mechanic | 5 | 15 | 8331-114 | Blacksmith | 5 | 15 |
| 9111-118 | Airline captain | 1 | 18 | 8581-142 | Body repairer | 1 | 15 |
| 2143-122 | Airport engineer | 5 | 18 | 9533-110 | Boiler operator | 5 | 15 |
| 8589-138 | Airport-maintenance worker | 5 | 15 | 9533-126 | Boiler operator, pulverised coal | 5 | 15 |
| 2119-120 | Alcohol examiner | 1 | 15 | 8584-148 | Boilerhouse repairer | 10 | 15 |
| 8584-202 | Ammunition-assembling-machine adjuster | 10 | 11 | 8337-110 | Boilermaker | 1 | 15 |
| 1176-154 | Ammunition-safety inspector | 5 | 11 | 8335-118 | Boilermaker, erection & repair | 1 | 15 |
| 2111-114 | Analytical chemist | 1 | 18 | 4131-114 | Bookkeeper | 1 | 11 |
| 2133-194 | Anatomist | 1 | 18 | 2351-120 | Bookmobile librarian | 3 | 11 |
| 2131-114 | Animal scientist | 1 | 18 | 2135-248 | Botanical technician | 1 | 11 |
| 3315-134 | Animation-camera operator | 1 | 15 | 2135-138 | Botanical technologist | 1 | 15 |
| 3314-114 | Animator | 3 | 15 | 2133-114 | Botanist | 1 | 18 |
| 3337-114 | Announcer | 1 | 15 | 8267-110 | Braid-pattern setter | 1 | 15 |
| 3337-110 | Announcer-producer international service | 1 | 15 | 1171-138 | Branch accountant, bank | 3 | 15 |
| 2313-110 | Anthropologists | 1 | 18 | 3337-116 | Broadcast journalist | 1 | 15 |
| 5199-122 | Antique dealer | 1 | 11 | 9551-114 | Broadcast transmitter operator | 5 | 15 |
| 8581-111 | Antique-car restorer | 1 | 18 | 9533-128 | Building systems technician | 5 | 11 |
| 2183-124 | Application programmer | 10 | 11 | 2143-126 | Buildings and bridge engineer | 5 | 18 |
| 2114-118 | Applications & impact meteorologist | 1 | 18 | 1171-186 | Bursar | 3 | 15 |
| 5199-110 | Appraiser | 1 | 15 | 4199-154 | Bus-transportation-service co-ordinator | 3 | 11 |
| 5199-118 | Appraiser, automobile | 1 | 11 | 5191-110 | Buyer | 1 | 15 |
| 2133-110 | Aquatic biologist | 1 | 18 | 8541-110 | Cabinetmaker | 1 | 15 |
| 2313-118 | Archaeologists | 1 | 18 | 8735-156 | Cable installer | 3 | 15 |
| 2141-110 | Architect | 1 | 18 | 8731-122 | Cable installer-repairer | 5 | 15 |

| CCDO Code | Detailed General Occupations List | Occupation Factor 4 points | SVP Factor 3 points | CCDO Code | Detailed General Occupations List | Occupation Factor 4 points | SVP Factor 3 points |
|---|---|---|---|---|---|---|---|
| 8739-130 | Cable splicer | 1 | 15 | 3137-117 | Community occupational therapist | 10 | 15 |
| 8736-114 | Cable tester | 5 | 15 | 2319-132 | Community recreation planner | 1 | 15 |
| 8735-170 | Cable-television installer | 3 | 11 | 2333-116 | Community-development worker | 5 | 11 |
| 2163-177 | CAD designer, printed circuit boards | 1 | 15 | 2331-114 | Community-organization worker | 5 | 18 |
| 8535-106 | CADD/CAM repair technician | 1 | 15 | 9533-134 | Compressor operator, caisson | 5 | 11 |
| 8213-110 | Cake decorator | 1 | 11 | 5131-116 | Computer consultant, market support | 1 | 15 |
| 3315-172 | Camera operator, motion picture | 1 | 15 | 8535-108 | Computer equip repair technician | 1 | 15 |
| 3315-170 | Camera operator, senior, motion picture | 1 | 15 | 2183-150 | Computer graphics specialist | 10 | 15 |
| 8588-126 | Camera repairer | 5 | 15 | 2183-154 | Computer hardware specialist | 10 | 15 |
| 1179-138 | Campaign consultant | 1 | 15 | 4143-110 | Computer operator | 1 | 11 |
| 8569-110 | Canvas worker | 1 | 15 | 2163-116 | Computer-assist design draughtsperson | 1 | 15 |
| 9135-114 | Car assignments clerk | 1 | 11 | 2351-121 | Computer-search librarian | 3 | 15 |
| 8583-110 | Car repairer | 1 | 15 | 4143-112 | Computerized information processor | 1 | 11 |
| 8311-134 | Carbide-tool maker | 5 | 15 | 1179-192 | Conference and meeting planner | 1 | 15 |
| 8581-150 | Carburetor repairer | 1 | 11 | 2353-128 | Conservation & restoration technician | 1 | 11 |
| 8584-230 | Card grinder | 10 | 11 | 6119-110 | Conservation officer | 3 | 11 |
| 2163-114 | Cartographer | 1 | 15 | 2351-166 | Conservator | 3 | 18 |
| 8584-206 | Carton-forming-machine repairer | 10 | 11 | 8584-378 | Construction equipment mechanic | 10 | 15 |
| 3314-140 | Cartoon background artist | 3 | 15 | 8537-112 | Consumer products service technician | 1 | 11 |
| 3314-134 | Cartoonist | 3 | 15 | 4139-110 | Contract clerk | 1 | 15 |
| 3319-228 | Carver, reproduction | 1 | 15 | 2349-118 | Contract clerk | 1 | 15 |
| 3330-130 | Casting officer | 3 | 15 | 1179-190 | Contracts administrator | 1 | 15 |
| 2351-126 | Cataloguer | 3 | 15 | 4151-122 | Control clerk, advertising | 1 | 11 |
| 2353-130 | Cataloguer, museum | 1 | 11 | 8588-112 | Control technician, nuc-gen & water plant | 5 | 15 |
| 6121-121 | Caterer | 10 | 18 | 8584-358 | Conveyor repairer | 10 | 11 |
| 2133-242 | Cell biologist | 1 | 18 | 6121-132 | Cook, camp | 10 | 15 |
| 8535-125 | Cellular telephone installer | 1 | 11 | 6121-118 | Cook, domestic | 10 | 15 |
| 6141-112 | Cemetery manager | 1 | 15 | 6121-127 | Cook, first | 10 | 15 |
| 9531-146 | Central office power room operator | 1 | 11 | 6121-126 | Cook, foreign foods | 10 | 15 |
| 8735-154 | Central-office-equipment installer | 3 | 11 | 6121-122 | Cook, institution | 10 | 15 |
| 8735-110 | Central-office-equipment repairer | 3 | 15 | 6121-124 | Cook, kosher foods | 10 | 15 |
| 2159-114 | Ceramics engineer | 5 | 18 | 6121-114 | Cook, small establishment | 10 | 15 |
| 8391-190 | Chaser | 1 | 11 | 6121-129 | Cook, therapeutic diet | 10 | 15 |
| 6121-120 | Chef, entremetier | 10 | 18 | 8333-114 | Coppersmith | 1 | 15 |
| 6121-119 | Chef, garde-manger | 10 | 18 | 4199-150 | Copy cutter | 3 | 18 |
| 6121-115 | Chef, patissier | 10 | 18 | 3319-166 | Copy stylist | 1 | 11 |
| 6121-117 | Chef, rotisseur | 10 | 18 | 1179-186 | Corporate planner | 1 | 15 |
| 6121-116 | Chef, saucier | 10 | 18 | 1179-178 | Corporate secretary | 1 | 18 |
| 6121-111 | Chef-cook, general | 10 | 15 | 2159-154 | Corrosion engineer | 5 | 18 |
| 2117-246 | Chem technician, heavy water plant & nuc-gen | 1 | 11 | 1179-204 | Cost estimator | 1 | 15 |
| 2142-110 | Chemical eng. design and development | 5 | 18 | 8553-174 | Costumer | 1 | 15 |
| 2142-118 | Chemical engineer, production | 5 | 18 | 2331-134 | Counsellor, addiction | 5 | 15 |
| 2142-114 | Chemical engineer, research | 5 | 18 | 2399-126 | Counsellor, attendance | 5 | 11 |
| 2111-118 | Chemical oceanographer | 1 | 18 | 2391-118 | Counsellor, educational | 1 | 15 |
| 2117-248 | Chemical technician | 1 | 11 | 2391-114 | Counsellor, general | 1 | 15 |
| 2117-110 | Chemical technologist | 1 | 15 | 2399-122 | Counsellor, marriage | 5 | 15 |
| 8584-138 | Chemical-process-equipment mechanic | 10 | 15 | 1174-132 | Counsellor, pre-retirement | 3 | 11 |
| 2359-114 | Chief conservator, art gallery | 1 | 18 | 2399-114 | Counsellor, rehabilitation | 5 | 15 |
| 3315-122 | Chief photographer | 1 | 15 | 2391-122 | Counsellor, vocational | 1 | 15 |
| 2154-110 | Chief-petroleum engineer | 5 | 18 | 4111-114 | Court reporter | 5 | 15 |
| 3339-118 | Chief-stage electrician | 1 | 15 | 9311-106 | Crane operator, drilling rig | 1 | 11 |
| 2333-115 | Child-care worker | 5 | 11 | 8584-354 | Crane repairer | 10 | 15 |
| 8739-114 | Circuit breaker mechanic | 1 | 15 | 1171-210 | Credit officer | 3 | 11 |
| 2143-118 | Civil engineer, general | 5 | 18 | 4169-114 | Credits-assessment clerk | 1 | 11 |
| 2165-222 | Civil engineering technician | 1 | 11 | 2119-112 | Crime detection lab analyst | 1 | 15 |
| 2165-122 | Civil engineering technologist | 1 | 15 | 3351-150 | Critic | 3 | 18 |
| 4192-110 | Claim adjuster | 3 | 15 | 3359-122 | Crossword puzzle maker | 1 | 11 |
| 4112-118 | Claim examiner | 3 | 15 | 2159-130 | Cryogenics engineer | 5 | 18 |
| 2114-114 | Climatologist | 1 | 18 | 8562-111 | Custom upholsterer | 1 | 15 |
| 2133-246 | Clinical chemist | 1 | 18 | 3156-112 | Cytogenetics technologist | 5 | 15 |
| 3137-116 | Clinical occupational therapy specialist | 10 | 15 | 3156-114 | Cytotechnologist | 5 | 15 |
| 2133-212 | Clinical pharmacologist | 1 | 18 | 8584-326 | Diary equipment repairer | 10 | 15 |
| 1179-162 | Co-ordinator, tourism | 1 | 15 | 3139-116 | Dance therapist | 1 | 15 |
| 2143-127 | Coastal engineer | 5 | 18 | 2181-126 | Demographer | 1 | 18 |
| 3319-134 | Colourist, photography | 1 | 11 | 3157-142 | Dental ceramist | 1 | 15 |
| 3351-166 | Columnist | 3 | 15 | 3157-110 | Dental hygienist | 5 | 11 |
| 3314-118 | Commercial artist | 3 | 15 | 3157-146 | Dental technician, crown and bridge | 1 | 15 |
| 3315-118 | Commercial photographer | 1 | 15 | 3157-138 | Dental technician, general | 1 | 15 |
| 8581-116 | Commercial transport vehicle mechanic | 1 | 15 | 3157-150 | Dental technician, metal | 1 | 15 |
| 3313-150 | Commercial-design artist | 1 | 15 | 3157-158 | Denture setter | 1 | 15 |
| 1179-149 | Community arts coordinator | 1 | 15 | 3157-126 | Denturist | 1 | 15 |

147

| CCDO Code | Detailed General Occupations List | Occupation Factor 4 points | SVP Factor 3 points | CCDO Code | Detailed General Occupations List | Occupation Factor 4 points | SVP Factor 3 points |
|---|---|---|---|---|---|---|---|
| 2144-110 | Design and development eng, electronic | 5 | 18 | 3351-202 | Editor, sports desk | 3 | 15 |
| 2163-118 | Design checker | 1 | 15 | 3351-138 | Editor, technical publication | 3 | 18 |
| 8391-122 | Design cutter, jewellery | 1 | 11 | 3351-186 | Editor, telecommunications | 3 | 15 |
| 8551-114 | Design & pattern maker, canvas goods | 1 | 11 | 3351-142 | Editor, trade or technical journal | 3 | 18 |
| 3313-166 | Designer, paper securities | 1 | 18 | 3353-110 | Editor, news, special events & public affairs | 1 | 18 |
| 2163-122 | Detail draughtsman/woman | 1 | 15 | 3351-194 | Editorial assistant | 3 | 11 |
| 2333-124 | Detention-home worker | 5 | 11 | 3351-170 | Editorial writer | 3 | 15 |
| 2311-122 | Development economist | 1 | 18 | 8739-122 | Electric-meter repairer | 1 | 15 |
| 3155-108 | Diagnostic medical sonographer | 5 | 15 | 2144-134 | Electrical & electronic aerospace eng. | 5 | 18 |
| 3155-114 | Diagnostic-radiological technician | 5 | 11 | 2144-118 | Electrical engineer, general | 5 | 18 |
| 8591-110 | Diamond cutter | 1 | 18 | 8533-110 | Electrical repairer | 1 | 15 |
| 8529-178 | Diamond-saw maker | 1 | 15 | 2165-226 | Electrical-engineering technician | 1 | 11 |
| 8311-114 | Diamond-tool maker | 5 | 15 | 2165-126 | Electrical-engineering technologist | 1 | 15 |
| 8585-122 | Dictating & transcribing machine servicer | 1 | 11 | 2144-138 | Electrical-equipment engineer | 5 | 18 |
| 8311-138 | Die finisher | 5 | 15 | 2144-142 | Electrical-systems planning engineer | 5 | 18 |
| 8311-118 | Die maker, bench, stamping | 5 | 15 | 8736-134 | Electrical testing technician | 5 | 11 |
| 8311-142 | Die maker, jewellery | 5 | 11 | 8736-110 | Electrical wiring inspector | 5 | 18 |
| 8399-116 | Die maker, paperboard | 1 | 15 | 8533-130 | Electrician, aircraft | 1 | 15 |
| 8311-122 | Die maker, wire-drawing | 5 | 15 | 8533-114 | Electrician, automotive | 1 | 15 |
| 8331-110 | Die setter | 5 | 15 | 8735-118 | Electrician, communications equipment | 3 | 15 |
| 8311-126 | Die sinker, bench | 5 | 15 | 8533-134 | Electrician, marine equipment | 1 | 15 |
| 9533-118 | Diesel engineer operator, stationary | 5 | 15 | 8739-110 | Electrician, powerhouse | 1 | 15 |
| 8584-382 | Diesel mechanic | 10 | 15 | 8533-138 | Electrician, rail transport | 1 | 15 |
| 9531-118 | Diesel plant operator | 1 | 15 | 8739-118 | Electrician, substation | 1 | 15 |
| 3152-122 | Dietitian | 1 | 15 | 2113-122 | Electricity & magnetism physicist | 1 | 18 |
| 3152-114 | Dietitian, consultant | 1 | 15 | 3159-138 | Electroencephalographic technician | 10 | 11 |
| 3152-126 | Dietitian, therapeutic | 1 | 15 | 3156-116 | Electron microscopy technologist | 5 | 15 |
| 1176-142 | Dining-service inspector | 5 | 11 | 8585-124 | Electronic cash register servicer | 1 | 11 |
| 3319-206 | Diorama maker | 1 | 11 | 2144-122 | Electronic engineer, general | 5 | 18 |
| 3330-158 | Director, broadcasting | 3 | 11 | 8535-136 | Electronic games repairer | 1 | 11 |
| 3330-150 | Director, motion picture | 3 | 18 | 8535-124 | Electronic music equip repairer | 1 | 11 |
| 3330-162 | Director, stage | 3 | 15 | 8535-105 | Electronic technician, drilling rig | 1 | 15 |
| 3319-202 | Display designer | 1 | 11 | 2165-230 | Electronic-engineering technician | 1 | 11 |
| 2144-130 | Distribution engineer | 5 | 18 | 2165-130 | Electronic-engineering technologist | 1 | 15 |
| 6199-110 | Diver | 1 | 11 | 2113-126 | Elementary-particle physicist | 1 | 18 |
| 2163-126 | Draughtsman/woman, architectural | 1 | 15 | 6141-114 | Embalmer | 1 | 11 |
| 2163-130 | Draughtsman/woman, civil | 1 | 15 | 3313-174 | Embroidery designer | 1 | 15 |
| 2163-134 | Draughtsman/woman, commercial | 1 | 15 | 1174-134 | Employment interviewer | 3 | 11 |
| 2163-138 | Draughtsman/woman, electrical | 1 | 15 | 1174-119 | Employment recruiter | 3 | 15 |
| 2163-140 | Draughtsman/woman, electro-mechanical | 1 | 15 | 9533-113 | Energy from waste plant operator | 5 | 15 |
| 2163-142 | Draughtsman/woman, electronic | 1 | 15 | 8592-134 | Engine fitter | 1 | 15 |
| 2163-150 | Draughtsman/woman, marine | 1 | 15 | 8581-114 | Engine repairer | 1 | 15 |
| 2163-154 | Draughtsman/woman, mechanical | 1 | 15 | 4199-164 | Engineering clerk | 1 | 11 |
| 2163-158 | Draughtsman/woman, mine | 1 | 15 | 1171-202 | Engineering-depreciation evaluator | 3 | 15 |
| 2163-162 | Draughtsman/woman, one-tenth scale | 1 | 15 | 8391-118 | Engraver, decorative | 1 | 15 |
| 2163-164 | Draughtsman/woman, petrol exploration | 1 | 15 | 8391-110 | Engraver, hand | 1 | 15 |
| 2163-168 | Draughtsman/woman, pipe organ | 1 | 15 | 8391-130 | Engraver, pantograph | 1 | 11 |
| 2163-170 | Draughtsman/woman, process piping | 1 | 15 | 2133-118 | Entomologist | 1 | 18 |
| 2163-146 | Draughtsman/woman, heating & ventilating | 1 | 15 | 2143-130 | Environmental engineer | 1 | 18 |
| 2163-110 | Draughtsman/woman, general | 1 | 15 | 2181-136 | Epidemiologist | 1 | 18 |
| 8589-118 | Dredge mechanic | 5 | 15 | 2353-126 | Equipment restorer | 1 | 11 |
| 8553-142 | Dressmaker | 1 | 18 | 4159-110 | Estimator, jewellery | 1 | 11 |
| 2165-225 | Drilling-fluid technician, offshore rig | 1 | 11 | 8736-130 | Exchange tester | 5 | 11 |
| 6169-110 | Dyer | 1 | 11 | 9111-122 | Executive pilot | 1 | 15 |
| 2133-130 | Ecologist | 1 | 18 | 4111-111 | Executive secretary | 5 | 15 |
| 2311-126 | Econometrician | 1 | 18 | 2359-110 | Exhibit designer, museum | 1 | 18 |
| 2311-114 | Economist, general | 1 | 18 | 3313-110 | Exhibition and display designer | 1 | 15 |
| 3351-114 | Editor, advertising | 3 | 18 | 2112-110 | Exploration geophysicist | 1 | 18 |
| 3351-110 | Editor, book | 3 | 18 | 2359-115 | Extension officer, museum | 1 | 15 |
| 3351-118 | Editor, city | 3 | 18 | 8311-146 | Extrusion-die template maker | 5 | 11 |
| 3353-114 | Editor, continuity & script | 1 | 18 | 8584-188 | Farm-equipment installer | 10 | 11 |
| 3351-190 | Editor, copy | 3 | 11 | 8584-330 | Farm-equipment mechanic | 10 | 15 |
| 3351-122 | Editor, editorial page | 3 | 18 | 9531-154 | Feeder-switchboard operator | 1 | 11 |
| 3351-126 | Editor, financial | 3 | 18 | 8584-210 | Fibreglass-forming-machine repairer | 10 | 11 |
| 3351-130 | Editor, magazine | 3 | 18 | 9531-144 | Field operator, nuclear-generating stn | 1 | 15 |
| 3351-206 | Editor, make-up | 3 | 11 | 2131-134 | Field service man | 1 | 18 |
| 2163-172 | Editor, map | 1 | 15 | 8589-110 | Field service representative | 5 | 15 |
| 3351-134 | Editor, news | 3 | 11 | 3330-174 | Film editor | 3 | 15 |
| 3351-210 | Editor, picture | 3 | 11 | 2311-130 | Financial economist | 1 | 18 |
| 3351-198 | Editor, special features | 3 | 15 | 1174-126 | Financial-aids officer | 3 | 15 |
| 3351-158 | Editor, sports | 3 | 15 | 6111-126 | Fire-fighter | 1 | 15 |

148

| CCDO Code | Detailed General Occupations List | Occupation Factor 4 points | SVP Factor 3 points | CCDO Code | Detailed General Occupations List | Occupation Factor 4 points | SVP Factor 3 points |
|---|---|---|---|---|---|---|---|
| 6111-122 | Fire-fighter, crash | 3 | 11 | 2119-116 | Hair & fibre examiner | 1 | 15 |
| 2159-148 | Fire-prevention engineer | 5 | 18 | 6143-118 | Hairdresser | 1 | 11 |
| 8526-154 | Firearms inspector | 1 | 11 | 2333-119 | Half-way house supervisor | 5 | 11 |
| 9111-119 | First officer | 1 | 15 | 8591-214 | Hammersmith | 1 | 11 |
| 2135-162 | Fish-farm technologist | 1 | 15 | 3313-178 | Handbag designer | 1 | 15 |
| 8226-111 | Fish-roe technician | 1 | 11 | 8599-214 | Harpsichord builder | 1 | 18 |
| 2133-150 | Fishery bacteriologist | 1 | 18 | 6121-112 | Head chef | 10 | 18 |
| 8335-122 | Fitter, structural metal | 1 | 15 | 1171-194 | Head office underwriter | 3 | 15 |
| 8275-110 | Fixer, boarding room | 1 | 11 | 2113-134 | Health physicist | 1 | 18 |
| 9113-114 | Flight dispatcher | 1 | 18 | 8535-142 | Hearing-aid repairer | 1 | 11 |
| 3319-230 | Floral arranger | 1 | 11 | 2147-126 | Heat-vent & air-conditioning engineer | 5 | 18 |
| 2113-130 | Fluids physicist | 1 | 18 | 8584-112 | Heavy-duty-equipment mechanic | 10 | 18 |
| 2797-122 | Flying instructor | 1 | 15 | 9111-126 | Helicopter pilot | 1 | 15 |
| 2797-126 | Flying instructor, helicopter | 1 | 15 | 2143-134 | Highway engineer | 5 | 18 |
| 2133-154 | Food bacteriologist | 1 | 18 | 3156-118 | Histology technologist | 5 | 15 |
| 2131-118 | Food scientist | 1 | 18 | 2319-114 | Historian | 1 | 18 |
| 2135-166 | Food technologist | 1 | 15 | 2117-232 | Holographic technician | 1 | 15 |
| 8226-110 | Food tester | 1 | 11 | 2319-134 | Home economics technologist | 1 | 15 |
| 1179-200 | Food-and-beverage controller | 1 | 11 | 2319-126 | Home economist | 1 | 18 |
| 1171-188 | Foreign banking arrangements officer | 3 | 15 | 2131-130 | Horticulturalist | 1 | 18 |
| 1171-206 | Foreign exchange trader | 3 | 15 | 3359-110 | Humourist | 1 | 15 |
| 3355-118 | Foreign-broadcast translator | 1 | 11 | 8526-258 | Hydraulic tester | 1 | 11 |
| 4135-186 | Foreign-remittance clerk | 1 | 11 | 8589-162 | Hydraulic-unit repairer | 5 | 11 |
| 3315-116 | Forensic photographer | 1 | 15 | 9531-138 | Hydro-electric-station operator | 1 | 15 |
| 2159-138 | Forest engineer | 5 | 18 | 2161-110 | Hydrographic surveyor | 1 | 15 |
| 2135-272 | Forest technician | 1 | 11 | 2112-122 | Hydrologist | 1 | 18 |
| 2117-114 | Forest-products technologist | 1 | 15 | 2117-256 | Hydrology technician | 1 | 11 |
| 2139-110 | Forester | 1 | 18 | 2399-130 | Hypnotherapist | 5 | 11 |
| 8584-150 | Forge-shop-machinery repairer | 10 | 11 | 2144-146 | Illuminating engineer | 5 | 18 |
| 1173-118 | Forms analyst-and-designer | 3 | 11 | 6143-112 | Image consultant | 1 | 11 |
| 3157-162 | Framework finisher, dentures | 1 | 11 | 3156-124 | Immunohematology technologist | 5 | 15 |
| 1179-202 | Freight-traffic consultant | 1 | 11 | 2133-156 | Immunologist | 1 | 18 |
| 8581-154 | Front-end aligner | 1 | 11 | 3156-123 | Immunology technologist | 5 | 15 |
| 8581-115 | Fuel system conversion installer | 1 | 15 | 2133-158 | Industrial bacteriologist | 1 | 18 |
| 8589-130 | Fuel-injection-unit servicer | 5 | 11 | 2311-134 | Industrial economist | 1 | 18 |
| 6141-110 | Funeral director | 1 | 15 | 2145-110 | Industrial engineering, general | 5 | 18 |
| 3313-130 | Fur designer | 1 | 18 | 5135-125 | Industrial engines and equip partsperson | 3 | 11 |
| 8555-118 | Fur-repair estimator | 1 | 11 | 2145-114 | Industrial hygienist | 5 | 18 |
| 3313-118 | Furniture designer | 1 | 18 | 1179-150 | Industrial-development representative | 1 | 15 |
| 8555-110 | Furrier, all round | 1 | 15 | 2165-238 | Industrial-engineering technician | 1 | 11 |
| 3313-134 | Garment designer | 1 | 18 | 2165-134 | Industrial-engineering technologist | 1 | 15 |
| 2159-126 | Gas and steam distribution engineer | 5 | 18 | 3313-138 | Industrial-products designer | 1 | 18 |
| 1176-150 | Gas-customer-liaison agent | 5 | 11 | 2145-118 | Industrial-safety engineer | 5 | 18 |
| 8588-134 | Gas-meter repairer | 5 | 11 | 8581-118 | Industrial-truck mechanic | 1 | 15 |
| 8536-154 | Gas-meter tester | 3 | 11 | 2359-118 | Information service worker, encyclopedia | 1 | 11 |
| 8316-118 | Gear inspector | 5 | 18 | 2111-122 | Inorganic chemist | 1 | 18 |
| 8591-118 | Gemmologist | 1 | 15 | 8536-130 | Inspector & tester, aircraft-electrical equip | 1 | 15 |
| 4135-110 | General clerk, insurance | 1 | 11 | 8536-134 | Inspector & tester, aircraft-electronic equip | 1 | 15 |
| 2133-250 | Geneticist | 1 | 18 | 8586-118 | Inspector, heavy equipment | 3 | 18 |
| 2319-110 | Geographer | 1 | 18 | 8316-114 | Inspector, machine shop | 5 | 15 |
| 2159-134 | Geological engineer | 5 | 18 | 8296-110 | Inspector, pharmaceuticals & toiletries | 1 | 15 |
| 2117-252 | Geological technician | 1 | 11 | 8596-180 | Inspector, returned materials | 1 | 11 |
| 2117-118 | Geological technologist | 1 | 15 | 8316-110 | Inspector, tool and gauge | 5 | 15 |
| 2165-234 | Geological-engineering technician | 1 | 11 | 1176-146 | Inspector, travel accommodation | 5 | 11 |
| 2112-114 | Geologist | 1 | 18 | 8226-120 | Inspector-grader, fish | 1 | 11 |
| 2117-276 | Geophysical technician | 1 | 11 | 8586-122 | Inspector/tester meteorological equip | 3 | 15 |
| 2117-122 | Geophysical technologist | 1 | 15 | 8535-118 | Installer & repairer, audio-visual equip | 1 | 11 |
| 2117-272 | Geophysical-equip. operator, airborne | 1 | 11 | 8635-130 | Installer & repairer, public address systems | 1 | 11 |
| 2112-118 | Geophysicist | 1 | 18 | 8533-154 | Installer & repairer, automatic-pinsetting machine | 1 | 11 |
| 2333-120 | Geriatric-activities aide | 5 | 11 | 8535-110 | Installer, aircraft electronic equip | 1 | 15 |
| 8155-230 | Glass blower | 1 | 15 | 8553-178 | Installer, household appliance | 1 | 11 |
| 8391-125 | Glass engraver | 1 | 11 | 8533-198 | Installer-servicer, dental equipment | 1 | 11 |
| 8155-234 | Glass-novelty maker | 1 | 11 | 2797-118 | Instructor, airline pilot | 1 | 18 |
| 5191-112 | Grain-elevator manager | 1 | 11 | 2797-146 | Instructor, auto driving | 1 | 11 |
| 1179-205 | Graphoanalyst | 1 | 15 | 2797-138 | Instructor, flight attendant | 1 | 15 |
| 8313-134 | Grinder set-up operator, jig | 1 | 15 | 2797-134 | Instructor, police | 1 | 15 |
| 2797-130 | Ground-school instructor | 1 | 15 | 8526-246 | Instrument inspector and tester | 1 | 15 |
| 2391-110 | Guidance head | 1 | 18 | 8313-138 | Instrument maker | 1 | 15 |
| 8584-154 | Gum-wrapping-machine mechanic | 10 | 11 | 2161-118 | Instrument man/woman | 1 | 15 |
| 8589-122 | Gunsmith | 5 | 15 | 8588-114 | Instrument mechanic, utilities | 5 | 15 |
| 8588-138 | Gyroscope repairer | 5 | 11 | 8588-118 | Instrument repairer | 5 | 15 |

149

| CCDO Code | Detailed General Occupations List | Occupation Factor 4 points | SVP Factor 3 points |
|---|---|---|---|
| 1176-114 | Insurance inspector, loss-prevention | 5 | 15 |
| 3313-114 | Interior designer and decorator | 1 | 18 |
| 2311-138 | International-trade economist | 1 | 18 |
| 1179-148 | Interpretation-visitor services coord | 1 | 15 |
| 3355-110 | Interpreter | 1 | 15 |
| 1171-184 | Investment analyst | 3 | 18 |
| 2143-138 | Irrigation and drainage engineer | 5 | 18 |
| 8591-122 | Jeweller | 1 | 15 |
| 8143-110 | Jewellery coverer | 1 | 11 |
| 8395-244 | Jig & form maker | 5 | 15 |
| 8549-302 | Jig builder | 1 | 11 |
| 8592-138 | Joiner | 1 | 15 |
| 8271-114 | Knitting-machine fixer | 1 | 11 |
| 8271-110 | Knitting-pattern setter | 1 | 15 |
| 2117-264 | Laboratory physical sciences technician | 1 | 11 |
| 2117-126 | Laboratory physical sciences technologist | 1 | 15 |
| 3156-130 | Laboratory technician, veterinary | 5 | 11 |
| 8256-110 | Laboratory tester | 1 | 11 |
| 2311-142 | Labour economist | 1 | 18 |
| 1174-110 | Labour-relations specialist | 3 | 18 |
| 2349-122 | Land-titles clerk | 1 | 11 |
| 2141-114 | Landscape architect | 1 | 18 |
| 8591-114 | Lapidary | 1 | 18 |
| 8335-119 | Laser-beam welder | 1 | 11 |
| 8584-214 | Laundry-machine mechanic | 10 | 11 |
| 2349-114 | Law clerk | 1 | 15 |
| 8541-114 | Lay-out marker | 1 | 15 |
| 8335-126 | Lay-out marker, structural metal | 1 | 15 |
| 3314-136 | Layout designer | 3 | 15 |
| 5135-111 | Leasing representative, motor vehicles | 3 | 11 |
| 4111-112 | Legal secretary | 5 | 11 |
| 8379-150 | Lens marker | 1 | 11 |
| 8373-206 | Lens-grinder-polisher setter | 1 | 15 |
| 3314-146 | Lettering artist | 3 | 11 |
| 3351-146 | Lexicographer | 3 | 18 |
| 2351-114 | Librarian | 3 | 15 |
| 2353-134 | Library technician | 1 | 15 |
| 3339-120 | Light technician | 1 | 15 |
| 8735-138 | Line installer-repairer | 3 | 15 |
| 8731-118 | Line maintainer | 5 | 15 |
| 8731-110 | Line maintainer, emergency service | 5 | 18 |
| 8731-126 | Line maintainer, street railway | 5 | 15 |
| 8731-114 | Line repairer | 5 | 15 |
| 2319-118 | Linguist | 1 | 18 |
| 3351-154 | Literary writer | 3 | 18 |
| 9531-110 | Load dispatcher | 1 | 18 |
| 8589-146 | Locksmith | 5 | 11 |
| 8523-114 | Locomotive builder | 1 | 15 |
| 9131-110 | Locomotive engineer | 1 | 15 |
| 8586-114 | Locomotive inspector | 3 | 18 |
| 8395-130 | Loftsman/woman (air/space craft) | 5 | 15 |
| 8592-110 | Loftsman/woman, (ship/boat building) | 1 | 18 |
| 2159-158 | Logging engineer, oil well | 5 | 18 |
| 8584-114 | Loom fixer | 10 | 15 |
| 8267-114 | Loom-pattern changer | 1 | 15 |
| 8271-118 | Looper fixer | 1 | 11 |
| 2147-130 | Lubrication engineer | 5 | 18 |
| 8523-118 | Machine builder | 1 | 15 |
| 8584-118 | Machine fixer, textile | 10 | 11 |
| 8584-238 | Machine-clothing replacer | 10 | 11 |
| 8313-146 | Machine-tool set-up operator | 1 | 15 |
| 8313-142 | Machine-tool setter | 1 | 15 |
| 8313-150 | Machinist, automotive | 1 | 15 |
| 8313-122 | Machinist, ballistics laboratory | 1 | 15 |
| 8313-110 | Machinist, experimental | 1 | 18 |
| 8313-154 | Machinist, general | 1 | 15 |
| 8313-126 | Machinist, model maker | 1 | 15 |
| 8313-158 | Machinist, motion picture equipment | 1 | 15 |
| 8585-110 | Mail-processing equip mechanic | 1 | 15 |
| 8586-138 | Maintenance analyst | 3 | 15 |
| 8313-162 | Maintenance machinist | 1 | 15 |

| CCDO Code | Detailed General Occupations List | Occupation Factor 4 points | SVP Factor 3 points |
|---|---|---|---|
| 8584-170 | Maintenance mechanic, compressed gas plant | 10 | 11 |
| 8626-250 | Major-assembly inspector | 1 | 11 |
| 6143-110 | Make-up artist | 1 | 11 |
| 1179-174 | Management-seminar leader | 1 | 18 |
| 1171-298 | Manager trainee, consumer credit | 3 | 11 |
| 3319-130 | Mannequin artist | 1 | 11 |
| 5133-110 | Manufacturers' agent | 1 | 15 |
| 2165-160 | Manufacturing cost estimator | 1 | 15 |
| 2145-126 | Manufacturing engineer | 5 | 18 |
| 2159-118 | Marine engineer | 5 | 18 |
| 4192-120 | Marine-cargo surveyor | 3 | 11 |
| 8592-202 | Marine-engine mechanic | 1 | 15 |
| 2311-158 | Market-research analyst | 1 | 15 |
| 8273-110 | Master dyer | 1 | 15 |
| 3337-122 | Master of ceremonies | 1 | 11 |
| 9551-110 | Master-control equipment operator | 5 | 15 |
| 8155-210 | Master-glass blower | 1 | 18 |
| 4151-114 | Material co-ordinator | 1 | 15 |
| 8596-184 | Materials & parts inspector | 1 | 11 |
| 2143-110 | Materials and testing engineer | 5 | 18 |
| 2311-146 | Mathematical economist | 1 | 18 |
| 2181-130 | Mathematician, applied | 1 | 18 |
| 2181-110 | Mathematician, research | 1 | 18 |
| 2147-118 | Mechanical engineer | 5 | 18 |
| 2147-134 | Mechanical engineer, gas utilization | 5 | 18 |
| 8484-132 | Mechanical maintainer, NUC-generating stn | 10 | 15 |
| 2165-246 | Mechanical-engineering technician | 1 | 11 |
| 2165-142 | Mechanical-engineering technologist | 1 | 15 |
| 8581-138 | Mechanical-unit repairer | 1 | 11 |
| 2113-138 | Mechanics physicist | 1 | 18 |
| 2133-162 | Medical bacteriologist | 1 | 18 |
| 3314-122 | Medical illustrator | 3 | 15 |
| 4111-113 | Medical secretary | 5 | 11 |
| 3156-122 | Medical-laboratory technologist | 5 | 15 |
| 5177-126 | Membership promotion officer | 1 | 11 |
| 8335-130 | Metal former, hand | 1 | 11 |
| 8339-130 | Metal-can machine setter | 1 | 11 |
| 2151-110 | Metallurgical-engineer | 5 | 18 |
| 2165-260 | Metallurgical-engineering technician | 1 | 11 |
| 8584-134 | Metalworking machinery mechanic | 10 | 15 |
| 2117-260 | Meteorological technician | 1 | 11 |
| 2114-110 | Meteorologist | 1 | 18 |
| 8736-122 | Meter tester | 1 | 15 |
| 1173-114 | Methods and procedures analyst | 3 | 15 |
| 2145-130 | Methods engineer | 5 | 18 |
| 2119-110 | Metallurgist, physical | 1 | 18 |
| 2165-228 | Metrology technician | 1 | 11 |
| 2133-168 | Microbiologist | 1 | 18 |
| 3156-126 | Microbiology technologist | 5 | 15 |
| 8557-110 | Milliner | 1 | 15 |
| 8584-122 | Millwright | 10 | 15 |
| 8584-350 | Mine-hoist repairer | 10 | 15 |
| 2112-126 | Mineralogist | 1 | 18 |
| 2183-158 | Minicomputer/microcomputer specialist | 10 | 15 |
| 2153-110 | Mining engineer | 5 | 18 |
| 2165-254 | Mining-engineering technician | 1 | 11 |
| 2165-150 | Mining-engineering technologist | 1 | SVP |
| 8584-174 | Mining-machinery mechanic | 10 | 11 |
| 1171-299 | Misc accountants, auditors & finance officers | 3 | 11 |
| 9551-122 | Mobile-broadcast-equipment installer | 5 | 15 |
| 9179-142 | Mobile-support equip operator | 1 | 11 |
| 8399-114 | Model and mock-up maker | 1 | 18 |
| 8395-118 | Model maker | 5 | 15 |
| 9599-114 | Model maker | 1 | 15 |
| 8333-122 | Model maker, fluorescent lightings | 1 | 15 |
| 8333-110 | Model maker, heating apparatus | 1 | 18 |
| 8395-134 | Model maker, jewellery | 5 | 15 |
| 8351-118 | Model maker, last | 5 | 11 |
| 8333-126 | Model maker, metal furniture | 1 | 11 |
| 8351-114 | Model maker, wood | 5 | 15 |
| 8395-200 | Model & mould maker, concrete prod | 5 | 15 |

150

| CCDO Code | Detailed General Occupations List | Occupation Factor 4 points | SVP Factor 3 points | CCDO Code | Detailed General Occupations List | Occupation Factor 4 points | SVP Factor 3 points |
|---|---|---|---|---|---|---|---|
| 2133-254 | Molecular biologist | 1 | 18 | 9551-199 | Other radio/TV broadcasting equip. operators | 5 | 15 |
| 9557-110 | Motion-picture projectionist | 1 | 11 | 2313-199 | Other sociologist, anthrplgst & social scientists | 1 | 18 |
| 4151-118 | Motor vehicle repair co-ordinator | 1 | 11 | 5131-199 | Other technical salespersons & related | 1 | 11 |
| 8581-110 | Motor-vehicle mechanic | 1 | 15 | 3355-199 | Other translators & interpreters | 1 | 11 |
| 8581-158 | Motorcycle repairer | 1 | 11 | 3351-299 | Other writers & editors, publication | 3 | 11 |
| 2165-162 | Mould designer | 1 | 15 | 3353-199 | Other writers & editors, radio, TV, theatre & film | 1 | 11 |
| 8395-204 | Mould maker | 5 | 11 | 8592-206 | Outboard-motor mechanic | 1 | 11 |
| 8311-112 | Mould maker | 5 | 15 | 1174-121 | Outplacement relocation specialist | 3 | 15 |
| 8137-130 | Moulder, bench | 10 | 11 | 8584-194 | Oven-equipment repairer | 10 | 11 |
| 3157-166 | Moulder, bench | 1 | 11 | 3313-154 | Package designer | 1 | 15 |
| 2359-116 | Museum educator | 1 | 15 | 8584-162 | Packaging-machine mechanic | 10 | 11 |
| 2353-132 | Museum technician | 1 | 11 | 8595-114 | Painter | 1 | 11 |
| 2351-119 | Music librarian | 3 | 15 | 2112-130 | Paleontologist | 1 | 18 |
| 3139-113 | Music therapist | 1 | 15 | 2133-258 | Parasitologist | 1 | 18 |
| 3330-154 | Musical director | 3 | 18 | 2331-118 | Parole officer | 5 | 15 |
| 8599-218 | Musical-instrument repairer | 1 | 18 | 1171-198 | Passenger and freight rates analyst | 3 | 15 |
| 2133-122 | Mycologist | 1 | 18 | 3319-162 | Paster, graphics | 1 | 11 |
| 8313-163 | NC machinist | 1 | 15 | 2349-110 | Patent agent | 1 | 18 |
| 8739-150 | Neon-sign erector | 1 | 11 | 2349-117 | Patent searcher | 1 | 15 |
| 8581-162 | New-car preparer | 1 | 11 | 2133-198 | Pathologist, animal | 1 | 18 |
| 3353-118 | News analyst, broadcasting | 1 | 18 | 2133-202 | Pathologist, medical | 1 | 18 |
| 3315-130 | News photographer | 1 | 15 | 2133-206 | Pathologist, plant | 1 | 18 |
| 3315-174 | News-camera operator | 1 | 15 | 9111-114 | Patrol, pilot | 1 | 15 |
| 2157-110 | Nuclear engineer | 5 | 18 | 8551-126 | Pattern modifier | 1 | 11 |
| 2113-142 | Nuclear physicist | 1 | 18 | 8551-118 | Patternmaker | 1 | 11 |
| 2165-258 | Nuclear-engineering technician | 1 | 11 | 8395-146 | Patternmaker, envelopes | 5 | 15 |
| 2165-154 | Nuclear-engineering technologist | 1 | 15 | 8395-154 | Patternmaker, hat | 5 | 15 |
| 3155-110 | Nuclear-medicine technician | 5 | 15 | 8313-114 | Patternmaker, metal | 1 | 18 |
| 2157-114 | Nuclear-operations engineer | 5 | 18 | 8395-128 | Patternmaker, metal | 5 | 15 |
| 9531-134 | Nuclear-reactor operator | 1 | 15 | 8395-138 | Patternmaker, metal furniture | 5 | 15 |
| 3152-118 | Nutritionist | 1 | 15 | 8395-142 | Patternmaker, pantograph machine | 5 | 15 |
| 1174-122 | Occupational Analyst | 3 | 15 | 8395-158 | Patternmaker, plaster | 5 | 11 |
| 3137-118* | Occupational therapist *see note at end of lis | 10 | 15 | 8551-122 | Patternmaker, shoe | 1 | 11 |
| 2143-128 | Ocean engineer | 5 | 15 | 8351-110 | Patternmaker, wood | 5 | 18 |
| 8585-118 | Office-machine repairer | 1 | 11 | 8562-112 | Patternmaker-and-upholsterer, aircraft | 1 | 15 |
| 3313-184 | Office-space planner | 1 | 15 | 5199-114 | Pawnbroker | 1 | 11 |
| 8584-178 | Oil-tool repairer | 10 | 11 | 1171-196 | Personal financial planner | 3 | 15 |
| 8584-139 | Open-end technician | 10 | 11 | 1174-118 | Personnel officer | 3 | 15 |
| 3139-111 | Operating room assistant | 1 | 11 | 2165-262 | Petrochemical-engineering technician | 1 | 11 |
| 2181-122 | Operations-research analyst | 1 | 18 | 2154-114 | Petroleum engineer | 5 | 18 |
| 8373-210 | Optician | 1 | 15 | 2112-134 | Petroleum geologist | 1 | 18 |
| 2113-146 | Optics physicist | 1 | 18 | 2133-170 | Pharmaceutical bacteriologist | 1 | 18 |
| 8584-128 | Ore-processing-equipment repairer | 10 | 15 | 5133-114 | Pharmaceutical representative | 1 | 11 |
| 8599-242 | Organ-pipe voicer | 1 | 15 | 3151-110 | Pharmacist, hospital | 1 | 18 |
| 2111-126 | Organic chemist | 1 | 18 | 3151-114 | Pharmacist, industrial | 1 | 18 |
| 1173-122 | Organizational analyst | 3 | 15 | 3151-118 | Pharmacist, retail | 1 | 18 |
| 3157-154 | Orthodontic technician | 1 | 15 | 2133-210 | Pharmacologist | 1 | 18 |
| 3157-170 | Orthodontic-band maker | 1 | 11 | 8558-130 | Photo-finishing-equipment repairer | 5 | 15 |
| 5174-199 | Other advertising sales occupations | 3 | 11 | 8585-120 | Photocopying-machine servicer | 1 | 11 |
| 3314-199 | Other advertising & illustrating artists | 3 | 11 | 8539-118 | Photoelectric-sorting-machine repairer | 1 | 11 |
| 2131-199 | Other agriculturalists & related scientists | 1 | 18 | 3315-110 | Photographer, general | 1 | 15 |
| 2183-199 | Other analysts, programmers & cryptanalysts | 10 | 11 | 2169-110 | Photogrammetist | 5 | 15 |
| 2133-299 | Other biologists & related scientists | 1 | 18 | 3319-126 | Photograph retoucher | 1 | 11 |
| 2142-199 | Other chemical engineers | 5 | 18 | 3315-120 | Photographic technician | 1 | 15 |
| 2111-199 | Other chemists | 1 | 18 | 2111-130 | Physical chemist | 1 | 18 |
| 2391-199 | Other comnty & social work related occups | 1 | 15 | 2113-150 | Physical oceanographer | 1 | 18 |
| 2311-199 | Other economists | 1 | 15 | 2133-214 | Physiologist | 1 | 18 |
| 2112-199 | Other geologists & related occupations | 1 | 18 | 3137-122 | Physiotherapist | 10 | 15 |
| 2145-199 | Other industrial engineers | 5 | 18 | 8599-230 | Piano repairer | 1 | 15 |
| 2359-198 | Other libr, musm & archival science occups | 1 | 11 | 8599-250 | Piano-tone regulator | 1 | 11 |
| 2343-199 | Other libr, musm & archival science techncns | 1 | 11 | 9111-112 | Pilot, general aviation | 1 | 15 |
| 2135-299 | Other life science technicians | 1 | 11 | 8313-130 | Pinion-and-wheel-cutting set-up operator | 1 | 11 |
| 2135-199 | Other life science technologists | 1 | 15 | 8592-122 | Pipe fitter | 1 | 15 |
| 2181-199 | Other mathematicians, statisticians & actuaries | 1 | 15 | 8523-130 | Pipe fitter, rail car & locomotive | 1 | 11 |
| 2319-199 | Other occupations in social science | 1 | 11 | 8523-118 | Pipe fitter, turbines | 1 | 15 |
| 1173-199 | Other organization & methods analysts | 3 | 11 | 8599-234 | Pipe-organ builder | 1 | 15 |
| 2154-199 | Other petroleum engineers | 5 | 18 | 8599-246 | Pipe-organ erector | 1 | 15 |
| 2113-199 | Other physicists | 1 | 18 | 8599-222 | Pipe organ tuner & repairer | 1 | 15 |
| 3330-199 | Other producers & directors, performing acts | 3 | 15 | 2143-142 | Pipeline engineer | 5 | 18 |
| 2315-199 | Other psychologists | 3 | 15 | 2319-142 | Planning technician | 1 | 11 |
| 1175-199 | Other purchasing officers & buyers | 1 | 15 | 7195-112 | Plant doctor | 1 | 11 |

| CCDO Code | Detailed General Occupations List | Occupation Factor 4 points | SVP Factor 3 points |
|---|---|---|---|
| 2144-150 | Plant engineer, electrical | 5 | 18 |
| 2131-122 | Plant scientist | 1 | 18 |
| 2113-154 | Plasma physicist | 1 | 18 |
| 8573-108 | Plastics moulding technician | 1 | 15 |
| 8584-140 | Plastics processing equipment mechanic | 10 | 11 |
| 8589-150 | Pneumatic-tool repairer | 5 | 11 |
| 8589-154 | Pneumatic-tube repairer | 5 | 11 |
| 8559-166 | Pneumatic-unit tester and repairer | 5 | 11 |
| 4135-114 | Policy-change clerk | 1 | 11 |
| 2319-122 | Political scientist | 1 | 18 |
| 2165-270 | Pollution control technician | 1 | 11 |
| 3315-126 | Portrait photographer | 1 | 15 |
| 8155-114 | Potter | 1 | 15 |
| 3313-158 | Pottery designer | 1 | 15 |
| 8584-182 | Powder-line repairer | 10 | 11 |
| 9533-122 | Power engineer, general | 5 | 15 |
| 2147-110 | Power engineer, mechanical | 5 | 18 |
| 9533-111 | Power engineer, automated control | 5 | 15 |
| 9531-130 | Power-control-room operator | 1 | 15 |
| 9531-122 | Power-switchboard operator | 1 | 15 |
| 8739-134 | Power-transformer repairer | 1 | 15 |
| 8584-130 | Powerhouse repairer | 10 | 15 |
| 8736-160 | Powerline patroller | 5 | 11 |
| 8591-126 | Precious stone setter | 1 | 15 |
| 8333-116 | Precision sheet metal fabricator | 1 | 15 |
| 2353-127 | Preparator | 1 | 11 |
| 2311-150 | Price economist | 1 | 18 |
| 8584-110 | Printing-machinery mechanic | 10 | 18 |
| 8735-158 | Private-branch-exchange installer | 3 | 11 |
| 8735-122 | Private-branch-exchange repairer | 3 | 15 |
| 2331-122 | Probation officer | 5 | 15 |
| 8535-109 | Process-control equip repairer | 1 | 15 |
| 3330-118 | Producer, broadcasting | 3 | 18 |
| 3330-110 | Producer, motion picture | 3 | 18 |
| 3330-114 | Producer, stage | 3 | 18 |
| 3339-126 | Production assistant | 3 | 11 |
| 4151-110 | Production co-ordinator | 1 | 15 |
| 2145-134 | Production engineer | 5 | 18 |
| 8535-146 | Production repairer | 1 | 11 |
| 4155-110 | Production-supply clerk | 3 | 11 |
| 3330-126 | Program co-ordinator, broadcasting | 3 | 15 |
| 3339-122 | Program planner, music | 1 | 15 |
| 3353-128 | Program researcher | 1 | 15 |
| 2183-118 | Programmer, business | 10 | 15 |
| 2183-130 | Programmer, detail | 10 | 11 |
| 2183-122 | Programmer, engineering and scientific | 10 | 15 |
| 9599-118 | Prop maker | 1 | 15 |
| 8316-122 | Propeller inspector | 5 | 11 |
| 1179-198 | Property administrator | 1 | 11 |
| 4135-118 | Property and equipment insurance clerk | 1 | 11 |
| 3339-110 | Property master | 1 | 15 |
| 2147-138 | Propulsion engineer, aerospace vehicles | 5 | 18 |
| 2119-118 | Prospector | 1 | 15 |
| 3159-110 | Prosthetist-orthotist | 10 | 18 |
| 8735-142 | Protective signal servicer | 3 | 11 |
| 8523-110 | Prototype builder | 1 | 18 |
| 2315-134 | Psychologist, clinical | 3 | 18 |
| 2315-138 | Psychologist, counselling | 3 | 18 |
| 2315-118 | Psychologist, developmental | 3 | 18 |
| 2315-122 | Psychologist, educational | 3 | 18 |
| 2315-126 | Psychologist, engineering | 3 | 18 |
| 2315-114 | Psychologist, experimental | 3 | 18 |
| 2315-110 | Psychologist, general | 3 | 18 |
| 2315-142 | Psychologist, industrial | 3 | 18 |
| 2315-146 | Psychologist, school | 3 | 18 |
| 2315-130 | Psychologist, social | 3 | 18 |
| 2315-150 | Psychometrist | 3 | 11 |
| 3337-126 | Public-address announcer | 1 | 11 |
| 1179-146 | Public-relations agent | 1 | 15 |
| 8589-126 | Pump installer & repairer | 5 | 11 |
| 8589-134 | Pump repairer | 5 | 15 |
| 1175-110 | Purchasing officer, business services | 1 | 15 |
| 1175-114 | Purchasing officer, food & related produce | 1 | 15 |
| 1175-118 | Purchasing officer, material | 1 | 15 |
| 2111-138 | Quality-control chemist | 1 | 18 |
| 2148-138 | Quality-control engineer | 5 | 18 |
| 1179-160 | Quantity surveyor | 1 | 18 |
| 8584-166 | Quilting-machine fixer | 10 | 11 |
| 1176-130 | Radiation-contamination monitor | 5 | 15 |
| 8537-114 | Radio servicer | 1 | 11 |
| 9916-110 | Radiographer, industrial | 3 | 11 |
| 3155-118 | Radiotherapy technician | 10 | 11 |
| 2143-146 | Railway engineer | 5 | 18 |
| 8586-142 | Railway-car inspector | 3 | 15 |
| 4139-114 | Rate reviewer | 1 | 11 |
| 9555-118 | Re-recording mixer | 5 | 15 |
| 3359-114 | Reader, first | 1 | 11 |
| 8584-218 | Record-process-equipment repairer | 10 | 11 |
| 1173-126 | Record-systems analyst | 3 | 15 |
| 3330-178 | Recording director | 3 | 18 |
| 8581-132 | Recreation vehicle repairer | 1 | 11 |
| 3139-114 | Recreational therapist | 1 | 15 |
| 2351-110 | Reference librarian | 3 | 15 |
| 2147-142 | Refrigeration engineer | 5 | 18 |
| 8533-118 | Refrigeration mechanic | 1 | 15 |
| 9533-114 | Refrigeration operator | 5 | 15 |
| 2399-118 | Rehabilitation specialist | 5 | 18 |
| 8739-126 | Relay tester-repairer | 1 | 15 |
| 3137-130 | Remedial gymnast | 10 | 11 |
| 2169-112 | Remote sensing technician | 5 | 15 |
| 8533-162 | Repairer, air-conditioner | 1 | 11 |
| 8535-138 | Repairer, automated-processing equip | 1 | 11 |
| 8533-122 | Repairer, electric motor | 1 | 15 |
| 8533-166 | Repairer, electric tool | 1 | 15 |
| 8533-142 | Repairer, electrical instruments | 1 | 15 |
| 8535-114 | Repairer, electronic equipment | 1 | 15 |
| 8533-126 | Repairer, major appliance | 1 | 15 |
| 8535-134 | Repairer, nucleonic-controller | 1 | 11 |
| 8533-170 | Repairer, portable appliance | 1 | 11 |
| 8585-114 | Repairer, punched-card machines | 1 | 11 |
| 8535-122 | Repairer, radio communication equip | 1 | 15 |
| 8533-150 | Repairer, refrigeration units | 1 | 11 |
| 8735-146 | Repairer, shop | 3 | 11 |
| 8589-144 | Repairer, small engines | 5 | 15 |
| 8533-174 | Repairer, storage battery | 1 | 11 |
| 8535-126 | Repairer, television-studio equip | 1 | 11 |
| 3351-174 | Reporter | 3 | 15 |
| 9919-108 | Research assistant | 1 | 11 |
| 2144-114 | Research eng, electrical & electronic | 5 | 18 |
| 3152-110 | Research nutritionist | 1 | 15 |
| 2339-110 | Research officer, social welfare | 5 | 18 |
| 4156-190 | Reserves clerk | 1 | 11 |
| 2154-118 | Reservoir engineer, petroleum | 5 | 18 |
| 5131-144 | Residential energy adviser | 1 | 11 |
| 2311-152 | Resource economist | 1 | 18 |
| 2135-268 | Resource management technician | 1 | 15 |
| 3159-134 | Respiratory technologist | 10 | 11 |
| 3351-182 | Rewriter | 3 | 15 |
| 8533-124 | Rig electrician | 1 | 15 |
| 8592-201 | Rig mechanic | 1 | 15 |
| 8592-130 | Rigger | 1 | 15 |
| 8535-107 | Robotics technician | 1 | 15 |
| 8584-242 | Roll builder | 10 | 11 |
| 8579-114 | Roller repairer | 1 | 11 |
| 8391-114 | Roller repairer, textile | 1 | 15 |
| 8263-110 | Rope-machine setter | 1 | 11 |
| 8313-174 | Rotary-head-milling machine set-up operator | 1 | 15 |
| 9179-114 | Route planning analyst | 1 | 11 |
| 8579-110 | Rubbering mechanic | 1 | 11 |
| 8569-114 | Rug repairer | 1 | 11 |
| 8735-114 | Rural telephone maintainer | 3 | 15 |
| 8589-142 | Safe-and-vault servicer | 5 | 15 |

| CCDO Code | Detailed General Occupations List | Occupation Factor 4 points | SVP Factor 3 points | CCDO Code | Detailed General Occupations List | Occupation Factor 4 points | SVP Factor 3 points |
|---|---|---|---|---|---|---|---|
| 1176-122 | Safety co-ordinator | 5 | 11 | 8592-126 | Shipfitter | 1 | 15 |
| 1176-110 | Safety inspector | 5 | 15 | 8592-114 | Shipwright, metal | 1 | 18 |
| 8551-110 | Sailmaker | 1 | 15 | 8592-118 | Shipwright, wood | 1 | 18 |
| 5131-110 | Sales engineer, light, heat and power | 1 | 18 | 3313-142 | Shoe designer | 1 | 18 |
| 5177-110 | Sales engineer, oil well services | 1 | 18 | 8561-114 | Shoe repairer | 1 | 15 |
| 5133-126 | Sales rep. commercial & industrial equip | 1 | 11 | 8561-110 | Shoemaker, custom | 1 | 15 |
| 5133-134 | Sales rep. garments & other textile prod | 1 | 11 | 8581-130 | Shop estimator | 1 | 15 |
| 5133-138 | Sales rep. motor vehicles and equipment | 1 | 11 | 3313-182 | Sign designer | 1 | 15 |
| 5133-150 | Sales rep. pulp and paper products | 1 | 11 | 3355-116 | Sign language interpreter | 1 | 15 |
| 5133-132 | Sales rep. wine, beer and spirits | 1 | 11 | 3319-114 | Signpainter | 1 | 15 |
| 5177-121 | Sales rep. freight forwarding services | 1 | 11 | 3319-170 | Sign-layout detailer | 1 | 15 |
| 5133-122 | Sales rep. canvas products | 1 | 11 | 2144-154 | Signal engineer | 5 | 18 |
| 5177-120 | Sales rep. employment services | 1 | 11 | 8735-130 | Signal maintainer | 3 | 15 |
| 5177-130 | Sales rep. financial services | 1 | 11 | 3319-226 | Silhouette artist | 1 | 11 |
| 5133-130 | Sales rep. food products | 1 | 11 | 8591-210 | Silversmith | 1 | 15 |
| 5177-122 | Sales rep. freight service | 1 | 11 | 2331-124 | Social worker | 5 | 15 |
| 5177-114 | Sales rep. hotel services | 1 | 15 | 2331-126 | Social worker, case work | 5 | 15 |
| 5131-146 | Sales rep. light, heat & power | 1 | 11 | 2331-130 | Social worker, group | 5 | 15 |
| 5133-142 | Sales rep. petroleum products | 1 | 11 | 2331-110 | Social-work supervisor | 5 | 18 |
| 5133-146 | Sales rep. plastic products | 1 | 11 | 2313-114 | Sociologists | 1 | 18 |
| 5177-134 | Sales rep. printing | 1 | 11 | 2133-174 | Soil bacteriologist | 1 | 18 |
| 5133-154 | Sales rep. rubber products | 1 | 11 | 2143-150 | Soil engineer | 5 | 18 |
| 5177-118 | Sales rep. telecommunications | 1 | 11 | 2131-126 | Soil scientist | 1 | 18 |
| 5133-118 | Sales rep. textbooks | 1 | 11 | 2113-158 | Solid state physicist | 1 | 18 |
| 1179-154 | Sales promotion administrator | 1 | 15 | 9555-110 | Sound mixer | 5 | 15 |
| 5174-118 | Salesperson, advertising | 3 | 11 | 9555-130 | Sound effects technician | 5 | 11 |
| 5174-110 | Salesperson, art | 3 | 15 | 2351-118 | Special librarian | 3 | 15 |
| 5135-121 | Salesperson, art | 3 | 11 | 3339-116 | Special-effects technician | 1 | 11 |
| 5135-116 | Salesperson, computers | 3 | 11 | 4135-122 | Special-endorsement clerk | 1 | 11 |
| 5135-118 | Salesperson, hearing aids | 3 | 11 | 3137-114 | Speech pathologist | 10 | 15 |
| 5135-120 | Salesperson, livestock | 3 | 11 | 8588-146 | Speedometer repairer | 5 | 11 |
| 5135-110 | Salesperson, motor vehicles | 3 | 11 | 3337-118 | Sports announcer | 1 | 11 |
| 5135-122 | Salesperson, musical instruments | 3 | 11 | 9111-134 | Spray pilot | 1 | 15 |
| 5135-126 | Salesperson, parts | 3 | 11 | 3330-166 | Stage manager | 3 | 15 |
| 5174-122 | Salesperson, radio or television time | 3 | 11 | 3339-124 | Stage production technician | 1 | 11 |
| 5135-114 | Salesperson, sewing machines | 3 | 11 | 3313-126 | Stained-glass artist | 1 | 18 |
| 5174-114 | Salesperson, signs and displays | 3 | 11 | 1173-112 | Standards specialist | 3 | 18 |
| 5135-124 | Salesperson, wood burning appliances | 3 | 11 | 9113-124 | Station agent | 1 | 15 |
| 8739-146 | Salvage repairer | 1 | 11 | 8735-126 | Station repairer | 3 | 15 |
| 8589-158 | Salvager, machinery | 5 | 11 | 1179-194 | Stations-relations administrator | 1 | 11 |
| 8313-166 | Sample maker, household appliances | 1 | 15 | 2189-114 | Statistical technician | 1 | 15 |
| 8395-114 | Sample maker, jewellery | 5 | 15 | 2181-134 | Statistician, applied | 1 | 18 |
| 8553-178 | Sample-garment maker | 1 | 11 | 2181-138 | Statistician, biological & agricultural | 1 | 18 |
| 8535-140 | Satellite antenna installer | 1 | 11 | 2181-142 | Statistician, business and economics | 1 | 18 |
| 8527-110 | Scale calibrator | 1 | 15 | 2181-114 | Statistician, mathematical | 1 | 18 |
| 8589-170 | Scale mechanic | 5 | 11 | 2181-146 | Statistician, physical science and eng. | 1 | 18 |
| 3319-110 | Scenery artist | 1 | 11 | 2181-150 | Statistician, social science | 1 | 18 |
| 9113-126 | Schedule analyst | 1 | 11 | 2181-154 | Statistician, vital | 1 | 18 |
| 3314-126 | Scientific illustrator | 3 | 15 | 9533-124 | Steam operator | 5 | 15 |
| 3315-14 | Scientific photographer | 1 | 15 | 8335-150 | Steel-plate shaper | 1 | 11 |
| 8155-212 | Scientific-glass-apparatus blower | 1 | 18 | 9555-114 | Stereo-tape editor | 5 | 15 |
| 3339-130 | Script assistant | 1 | 11 | 2169-118 | Stereoplotter | 5 | 18 |
| 3353-130 | Script reader | 1 | 11 | 4155-111 | Storekeeper, drilling rig | 3 | 11 |
| 3353-122 | Script writer | 1 | 15 | 3314-112 | Story board artist | 3 | 15 |
| 8584-222 | Seamer-machine repairer | 10 | 11 | 8583-114 | Streetcar and subway-car mechanic | 1 | 15 |
| 9111-136 | Second officer | 1 | 15 | 8549-222 | Stringed-instrument maker | 1 | 18 |
| 4111-110 | Secretary | 5 | 11 | 8549-226 | Stringed-instrument repairer | 1 | 15 |
| 1171-182 | Securities counsellor | 3 | 18 | 2143-114 | Structural-design engineer | 5 | 18 |
| 8535-127 | Security alarm installer | 1 | 11 | 8335-114 | Structural-metal fabricator | 1 | 15 |
| 2112-138 | Seismologist | 1 | 18 | 1171-200 | Student awards officer | 3 | 15 |
| 4192-114 | Service representative | 3 | 11 | 2339-114 | Student-activities adviser | 5 | 11 |
| 1179-134 | Service-station inspector | 5 | 15 | 9531-114 | Substation inspector | 1 | 11 |
| 3313-122 | Set designer | 1 | 18 | 9199-112 | Subway-traffic controller | 1 | 11 |
| 8533-146 | Sewer | 1 | 11 | 4199-162 | Suggestion-program clerk | 3 | 11 |
| 8553-150 | Sewer, women's garment alterations | 1 | 11 | 1171-110 | Supervisor, accountants | 3 | 18 |
| 2797-128 | Sewing instructor | 1 | 15 | 3314-110 | Supervisor, art | 3 | 15 |
| 8584-198 | Sewing-machine mechanic | 10 | 11 | 1171-158 | Supervisor, auditors | 3 | 18 |
| 8584-234 | Shearing-machine fixer | 10 | 11 | 2311-110 | Supervisor, economic research | 1 | 18 |
| 8333-130 | Sheet-metal layout detailer | 1 | 11 | 1173-110 | Supervisor, organization analysts | 3 | 18 |
| 8333-118 | Sheet-metal worker | 1 | 11 | 3139-110 | Surgical assistant | 1 | 11 |
| 2159-122 | Ship-construction engineer | 5 | 18 | 8588-122 | Surveying & optical instrument repairer | 5 | 15 |

153

| CCDO Code | Detailed General Occupations List | Occupation Factor 4 points | SVP Factor 3 points | CCDO Code | Detailed General Occupations List | Occupation Factor 4 points | SVP Factor 3 points |
|---|---|---|---|---|---|---|---|
| 2161-114 | Surveyor | 1 | 15 | 3355-122 | Translator | 1 | 11 |
| 9551-126 | Switcher | 5 | 15 | 3355-114 | Translator, scientific documents | 1 | 15 |
| 2183-110 | Systems analyst business, E.D.P. | 10 | 18 | 2144-162 | Transmission engineer | 5 | 18 |
| 2183-114 | Systems analyst engineering-scientific | 10 | 18 | 8581-122 | Transmission mechanic | 1 | 15 |
| 2183-116 | Systems-software programmer | 10 | 15 | 8736-142 | Transmission tester | 5 | 11 |
| 8553-110 | Tailor, made-to-measure garments | 1 | 18 | 2311-156 | Transport economist | 1 | 18 |
| 8553-118 | Tailor, mens garment alterations | 1 | 11 | 1179-140 | Travel agent | 1 | 15 |
| 8553-114 | Tailor, ready-to-wear garments | 1 | 11 | 8658-186 | Treatment-plant mechanic | 10 | 11 |
| 8584-158 | Tannery-machinery repairer | 10 | 11 | 7195-110 | Tree surgeon | 1 | 11 |
| 8226-194 | Taster & buyer, beverages | 1 | 15 | 8581-126 | Trolley coach mechanic | 1 | 15 |
| 2311-154 | Tax economist | 1 | 18 | 8581-140 | Truck-trailer repairer | 1 | 15 |
| 2353-118 | Taxidermist | 1 | 15 | 1171-190 | Trust officer | 3 | 15 |
| 8587-114 | Taximeter repairer | 1 | 11 | 8581-134 | Tune-up specialist | 1 | 11 |
| 2333-117 | Teaching homemaker | 5 | 11 | 8511-110 | Turbine fitter | 1 | 18 |
| 2163-176 | Technical illustrator | 1 | 15 | 9531-142 | Turbine operator, steam | 1 | 15 |
| 3330-122 | Technical producer | 3 | 18 | 8313-118 | Turbine-blade fitter | 1 | 15 |
| 5131-122 | Technical salesperson, agricultural equip | 1 | 15 | 8155-218 | Undermaster glass blower | 1 | 18 |
| 5131-118 | Technical salesperson, aircraft | 1 | 15 | 8562-110 | Upholsterer, all around | 1 | 15 |
| 5131-150 | Technical salesperson, chemicals | 1 | 11 | 2319-130 | Urban & regional planner | 1 | 18 |
| 5131-114 | Technical salesperson, E.D.P. | 1 | 18 | 4135-182 | Utility clerk, bank | 1 | 11 |
| 5131-130 | Technical salesperson, electronic equip | 1 | 15 | 8562-114 | Vehicle upholstery repairer | 1 | 15 |
| 5131-132 | Technical salesperson, heavy equipment | 1 | 15 | 3115-110 | Veterinarian | 1 | 18 |
| 5131-134 | Technical salesperson, industrial equip | 1 | 15 | 8535-123 | Video equipment repairer | 1 | 11 |
| 5131-138 | Technical salesperson, medical-dental equip | 1 | 15 | 9555-122 | Video-and-sound recorder | 5 | 15 |
| 5131-154 | Technical salesperson, metals | 1 | 11 | 9551-118 | Video console operator | 5 | 15 |
| 5131-142 | Technical salesperson, railroad equip | 1 | 15 | 9555-126 | Video-recording-equipment operator | 5 | 15 |
| 5131-126 | Technical salesperson, construction equip | 1 | 15 | 3314-135 | Videotex page designer | 3 | 15 |
| 4111-115 | Technical secretary | 5 | 11 | 2133-244 | Virologist | 1 | 18 |
| 3351-178 | Technical writer | 3 | 15 | 2135-148 | Virology technologist | 1 | 15 |
| 1179-158 | Technical-service consultant | 1 | 15 | 8739-154 | Voltage-regulator maintainer | 1 | 11 |
| 2183-162 | Telecommunications specialist computers | 10 | 15 | 3339-114 | Wardrobe supervisor | 1 | 15 |
| 8735-166 | Telecommunications equipment installer | 3 | 11 | 8587-110 | Watch repairer | 1 | 15 |
| 8735-134 | Telegraph-equipment repairer | 3 | 15 | 2117-244 | Water-purification technician | 1 | 15 |
| 2144-168 | Telephone engineer | 5 | 18 | 2143-154 | Water-resource engineer | 5 | 18 |
| 8735-162 | Telephone-station installer | 3 | 11 | 2114-122 | Weather forecaster | 1 | 18 |
| 8537-110 | Television repair servicer | 1 | 15 | 8336-110 | Weld inspector | 1 | 15 |
| 3315-178 | Television-camera operator | 1 | 15 | 8335-110 | Welder setter, resistance | 1 | 15 |
| 8395-150 | Template maker | 5 | 15 | 8335-138 | Welder, arc | 1 | 15 |
| 8526-274 | Tensile-strength tester | 1 | 11 | 8335-126 | Welder, combination | 1 | 15 |
| 8736-138 | Terminal and repeater tester | 5 | 11 | 8335-112 | Welder, drilling rig | 1 | 15 |
| 9111-110 | Test pilot | 1 | 18 | 8335-142 | Welder, gas | 1 | 11 |
| 8539-114 | Test-equip repairer, oil exploration | 1 | 15 | 8335-120 | Welder, pipeline | 1 | 15 |
| 8736-126 | Tester and regulator | 5 | 15 | 8335-122 | Welder, pressure vessels | 1 | 15 |
| 8586-126 | Tester, automotive vehicle | 3 | 15 | 8335-118 | Welder, tool and die | 1 | 15 |
| 8536-110 | Tester, control-panel | 1 | 18 | 8335-114 | Welder-fitter | 1 | 15 |
| 8536-122 | Tester, systems | 1 | 15 | 2159-142 | Welding engineer | 5 | 18 |
| 9916-114 | Tester, ultrasonic | 3 | 11 | 8335-334 | Welding technician | 1 | 15 |
| 3313-146 | Textile designer | 1 | 18 | 8584-190 | Welding-equipment repairer | 10 | 15 |
| 2117-268 | Textile technician | 1 | 11 | 8335-134 | Welding-machine operator, submerged arc | 1 | 11 |
| 2117-130 | Textile technologist | 1 | 15 | 8335-130 | Welding-machine operator, gas-shielded arc | 1 | 11 |
| 2113-162 | Thermal physicist | 1 | 18 | 8586-150 | Wheel and axle inspector | 3 | 11 |
| 2145-122 | Time-study engineer | 5 | 18 | 8599-238 | Wind instrument repairer | 1 | 15 |
| 8395-208 | Tire-mould repairer | 5 | 15 | 8533-146 | Wirer & repairer, office machines | 1 | 15 |
| 2349-126 | Title examiner | 1 | 11 | 3313-162 | Women's fashion designer | 1 | 15 |
| 8584-226 | Tobacco-machine adjuster | 10 | 11 | 8549-246 | Wood carver | 1 | 18 |
| 8311-110 | Tool and die maker | 5 | 15 | 8585-121 | Word & info processing equip servicer | 1 | 11 |
| 2147-114 | Tool engineer | 5 | 18 | 1173-130 | Work-study analyst | 3 | 11 |
| 8311-130 | Tool maker, bench | 5 | 15 | 6121-123 | Working sous-chef | 10 | 18 |
| 2183-126 | Tool programmer, numerical control | 10 | 18 | 3353-126 | Writer, news/script, international broadcasting | 1 | 15 |
| 9599-110 | Totalizer-systems analyst | 1 | 18 | 9131-114 | Yard engineer | 1 | 11 |
| 1179-139 | Tour operator | 1 | 15 | 2135-252 | Zoological technician | 1 | 11 |
| 2133-213 | Toxicologist | 1 | 18 | 2135-142 | Zoological technologist | 1 | 15 |
| 2349-115 | Trademark agent | 1 | 15 | 2133-126 | Zoologist | 1 | 15 |
| 2159-150 | Traffic engineer | 5 | 18 | | | | |
| 1176-126 | Traffic inspector | 5 | 11 | | | | |
| 9113-128 | Traffic technician | 1 | 11 | | | | |
| 8739-162 | Traffic-light installer | 1 | 11 | | | | |
| 9135-110 | Train dispatcher | 1 | 15 | | | | |
| 2797-142 | Training representative | 1 | 15 | | | | |
| 2797-120 | Training specialist, computers | 1 | 15 | | | | |
| 8739-138 | Transformer repairer | 1 | 15 | | | | |

3137-118*  Occupational Therapist – This is a designated occupation. If you intend to settle in Alberta or Ontario and your qualifications have been formally assessed as acceptable by the relevant authorities in the province where you will reside: You will receive additional points as described in this guide under factors 4 & 5 for designated occupation. This only applies to occupational therapists destined for Alberta and Ontario.

# Glossary

**Anglophone**. A native English speaker. Geographical areas can also be referred to as Anglophone or Francophone.

**CCIP**. Canada Career Information Partnership, a national network of government and private sector agencies which provide career and labour market information to Canadians. See Useful Addresses for contact details.

**CEC**. Canada Employment Centre. Located in cities and towns throughout Canada, these offices are where one registers for a Social Insurance Number. They also provide help with job hunting.

**Chronological CV/résumé**. Shows job experience and educational qualifications in date order (from the most recent to the oldest).

**College**. Post-secondary education, not as advanced as university.

**E-mail**. Part of the Internet which allows messages to be sent to and received by individuals with addresses on the system.

**Employment Authorisation**. A work permit. Issued by the Canadian High Commission.

**Federal government**. The government of Canada, responsible for country-wide taxation, defence, budgets, law and order.

**Francophone**. A native French speaker. Geographical areas can also be referred to as Francophone or Anglophone.

**Functional CV/résumé**. Classifies job experience and educational qualifications by skills.

**Gas**. Petrol, when used with reference to automobiles.

**Governor General of Canada**. Represents the Queen in Canadian government, signing Acts of Parliament.

**High school**. Post-secondary education. Completed before college and/or university.

**House of Commons**. Elected body of Members of Parliament. Fulfils the same function as the House of Commons in Britain.

**Immigration attorney**. A solicitor who specialises in legal matters pertaining to immigration and offers services to help intending immigrants obtain employment authorisation and/or Landed Immigrant status.

**Immigration consultant**. Offers services designed to help the intending immigrant obtain employment authorisation and/or Landed Immigrant status and, sometimes, to settle in the new country.

**Internet.** The world-wide system of electronic communication via computer links.

**Landed Immigrant.** Someone who has been granted immigrant status and is entitled to live and work in Canada as a permanent resident.

**Medicare.** A name often given to the various provincial health insurance schemes.

**Province.** One of the ten separate areas of Canada which enjoy a degree of self-government. Similar to English counties.

**Provincial government.** The more localised elected government responsible for local taxes, health care, transportation.

**Real estate.** Land and/or property available to buy and sell. A real estate agent is called an estate agent in the UK.

**Résumé** A North American term for a CV.

**Senate.** A Canadian federal government body, corresponds to the British House of Lords.

**SIN.** An abbreviation of Social Insurance Number, without which one cannot work legally in Canada. Similar to the British National Insurance number.

**Sponsor.** A Canadian citizen or permanent resident who is willing to financially support an intending immigrant or temporary worker.

**Territory.** Similar to a province (see above), exercising a degree of self-government. There are two Territories in Canada.

**UIC.** Unemployment Insurance Commission. The government body which controls unemployment benefits (these are also referred to by the initials UIC).

**Vacation.** Holiday.

**Visa officer.** The immigration official who deals with individual applications.

**WWW.** World Wide Web. The interactive part of the Internet, containing a plethora of generally uncategorised information.

# Further Reading

## ABOUT CANADA

*Canada: A Portrait* (Ministry of Supply and Services, Canada).
*Canada the Culture*, Bobbie Kalman (Crabtree, 1993).
*Canada the People*, Bobbie Kalman (Crabtree, 1993).
*Canada: The Rough Guide*, Tim Jepson, Phil Lee, Tania Smith (Rough Guides, 1992).
*Canada Year Book* (Statistics Canada, 1994).
*Canadian Almanac and Directory* (Canadian Almanac and Directory, 1995).
*Canadian Key Business Directory* (Dun and Bradstreet Canada, 1992).
*Journey Through Canada*, Richard Tames (Eagle, 1991).
*The Moneywise Guide to North America*, Alla L Crew and Nicholas H Ludlow (BUNAC, 1992).
*Penguin Guide to Canada* (Penguin, 1990).
*The School Solution* (Canada Information Services, 1995).
*U-Choose – A Guide to Canadian Universities* (Moving Publishers Ltd, Canada).

## EMPLOYMENT INFORMATION

*Action Careers: Employment in the High Risk Job Market* (1987).
*(The) Ayer Directory of Publications* (Ayer, Canada, 1994).
*Benn's Media Directory* (Canada, 1994).
*Canadian Franchise Guide Vol 3*, J White.
*Canada's Best Careers Guide*, Frank Feather (Warwick Publishing, 1994).
*(The) Canada Contact Directory* (The Expat Network).
*(The) Canadian Key Business Directory* (Canada, 1994).
*CANTECH National Directory* (CANTECH, Canada).
*(The) CEPEC Recruitment Guide* (CEPEC, annual).
*Directory of Assessment and Development Consultants* (Executive Grapevine, annual).
*Directory of Associations in Canada* (Canada, 1994).
*Directory of Canadian Manufacturers* (Canada, 1994).
*Directory of Executive Recruitment Consultants* (Executive Grapevine, annual).
*Directory of Jobs and Careers Abroad*, A deVries (Vacation Work).

*Enterprising Canadians – the self-employed in Canada* (Statistics Canada, 1994).

*Evaluating Franchise Opportunities*, D Lunny.

*Excelerate*, Nuala Beck (Harper Collins Publishing Ltd, 1995).

*Finding Work Overseas*, Mathew Cunningham (How To Books, 1996).

*How to Emigrate*, Roger Jones (How To Books, 1994).

*How to Find Temporary Work Abroad*, Nick Vandome (How To Books).

*How to Get a Job Abroad*, Roger Jones (How To Books, 4th edition 1995).

*(The) Infomedia Revolution*, Frank Koelesch (McGraw Hill Ryerson, 1995).

*Live & Work in Canada*, Avril Harper (Grant Dawson, 1992).

*Live and Work in the USA and Canada*, Adam Lechmere (Vacation Work, 1995).

*Market Research Handbook* (Statistics Canada, annual).

*Megatrends 200: Ten New Directions for the 1990s* (1990).

*Obtaining Visas & Work Permits*, Roger Jones (How To Books, 1996).

*Summer Jobs Abroad*, D Woodworth (Vacation Work).

*Summer Jobs USA* (Peterson's Guide, 1996).

*What Color is Your Parachute?*, Richard Nelson Bolles (Ten Speed Press, 1995).

*Where the Jobs Are*, Colin Campbell (Macfarlane Walter and Ross, 1994).

*Who Owns Whom* (Dun and Bradstreet UK, annual).

*Willing's Press Guide* (1004, Canada).

*Working Abroad – the Daily Telegraph guide to working and living overseas*, Godfrey Golzen (Kogan Page, London, annual).

*Working Holidays*, Sewell (Central Bureau).

*Working Holidays Abroad*, Mark Hempshell (Kuperard).

*Working in Canada*, Johnson and Walter (Black Rose Books, Canada).

*Working on Contract Worldwide*, Rod Briggs (How To Books, 1996).

*Working in Ski Resorts*, Pybus (Vacation Work).

*Working on Contract Worldwide: how to triple your earnings by working as an independent contractor anywhere in the world*, Rod Briggs (How To Books, 1996).

*(The) Yearbook of Recruitment and Employment Services*, (UK, annual).

# Useful Addresses

## AGENTS-GENERAL FOR CANADIAN PROVINCES LOCATED IN THE UK

Agent-General for Alberta, 1 Mount Street, London W1Y 5AA.
Agent-General for British Columbia, 1 Regent Street, London SW1Y 4NS.
Agent-General for Nova Scotia, 14 Pall Mall, London SW1Y 5LU.
Agent-General for Ontario, 21 Knightsbridge, London SW1X 7LY.
Agent-General for Québec, 59 Pall Mall, London SW1 5JH.
Agent-General for Saskatchewan, 16 Berkeley Street, London W1X 5AE.

## BETTER BUSINESS BUREAUX

Better Business Bureau of:

**Calgary and Southern Alberta**. #350, 7330 Fisher Street, SE Calgary, AB T2H 2H8. Tel: (403) 258 2920.
**Central and Northern Alberta**. Capitol Place, #514, 9707 – 110 Street, Edmonton, AB T5K 2L9. Tel: (403) 482 2341.
**Mainland of British Columbia**. #404, 788 Beatty Street, Vancouver, BC V6B 2M1. Tel: (604) 682 2711. Fax: (604) 681 1544.
**Metropolitan Toronto Inc**. #403, 1 St John's Road, Toronto, ON M6P 4C7. Tel: (416) 766 5744. Fax: (416) 767 1970.
**Midwestern Ontario**. 220 Charles Street, Kitchener, ON N2G 2P7. Tel: (519) 579 3080.
**New Brunswick**. #313, 236 St George Street, PO Box 1002, Moncton, NB E1C 8P2. Tel: (505) 857 3255.
**Newfoundland and Labrador Ltd**. 360 Topsail Road, St John's, NF A1E 2B6. Tel: (709) 364 2222.
**Nova Scotia**. 1731 Barrington Street, Halifax, NS B3J 2A4. Tel: (902) 422 6581.
**Ottawa and Hull Inc**. #503, 71 Bank Street, Ottawa, ON K1P 5N2. Tel: (613) 237 4856.
**Saskatchewan Inc**. 1601 McAra Street, 2nd Floor, Regina, SK S4N 6H4. Tel: (306) 352 7601.
**South Central Ontario**. 50 Bay Street South, Hamilton, ON L8P 4V9. Tel: (416) 526 1111. Fax: (416) 526 1225.

**Vancouver Island.** #201, 1005 Langley Street, Victoria, BC V8W 1V7. Tel: (604) 386 6348.

**Western Ontario.** #402, 700 Richmond Street, London ON N6A 5C7. Tel: (519) 673 3222.

**Windsor and District.** 500 Riverside Drive West, Windsor, ON N9A 5K4. Tel: (519) 258 7222.

**Winnipeg and Manitoba Inc.** #204, 365 Hargrave Street, Winnipeg, MB R3B 2K3. Tel: (204) 943 1486. Fax: (204) 943 1489.

**Montreal Inc.** (Bureau d'Ethique Commerciale de Montréal Inc), #460, 2055 rue Péel, Montréal, PQ H3A 1V4. Tel: (514) 286 9281. Fax: (514) 849 7402.

**Québec Inc.** (Bureau d'Ethique Commerciale de Québec Inc), 485 rue Richelieu, Québec, PQ G1R 1K2. Tel: (418) 523 2555.

## CANADA CAREER INFORMATION PARTNERSHIP OFFICES (CCIPS)

### Canada CIP

Occupational and Career Development Division, Human Resources Development Canada, 5th Flr, Phase IV, 140 Promenade du Portage, Hull, PQ KA1 0J9.

### Provincial and Territorial CIPs

**Alberta.** Advanced Education and Career Development, 8th Flr, 10155–102 Street, Edmonton, AB T5J 4L5.

**British Columbia.** Labour Market Career Information Consortium, 5050 Kingsway, 6th Flr, Burnaby, BC V5H 4C3.

**Manitoba.** Manitoba Education and Training, W150–1970 Ness Avenue, Winnipeg, MN R3J 0Y9.

**New Brunswick.** Human Resources Development New Brunswick, Programs Branch, PO Box 6000, Fredericton, NB E3B 5H1.

**Newfoundland.** Career Support Services, Employment and Careers Branch, Department of Employment and Labour Relations, PO Box 8700, St John's, NF A1B 4J6.

**Northwest Territories.** Career and Employment Development Branch, NWT Education Culture and Employment, PO Box 1320, Yellowknife, NWT X1A 2L9.

**Nova Scotia.** Career Services Branch, Department of Education, PO Box 578, 2021 Brunswick Street, Halifax, NS B3A 1J8.

**Ontario.** Ministry of Education and Training, 900 Bay Street, 16th Flr, Mowat Block, Toronto, ON M7A 1L2.

**Prince Edward Island.** Department of Education, PO Box 2000, Charlottetown, PEI C1A 7N8.

**Saskatchewan.** Career Services, Saskatchewan Education Training and Employment, 2220 College Avenue, Regina, Sask S4P 3V7.

**Yukon.** CIP Coordinator, F H Collins Secondary School, 1001 Lewes

Boulevard, Whitehorse, YT Y1A 3J1.

## CHAMBERS OF COMMERCE

London Chamber of Commerce, 69 Cannon Street, London EC4N 5AB. Tel: (0171) 248 4444. Canada/UK Chamber of Commerce, 3 Regent Street, London SW1Y 4NZ. Tel: (0171) 930 7711. Canadian Chamber of Commerce, 55 Metcalfe Street, # 1160, Ottawa, ON K1P 6N4.

## CREDENTIAL ASSESSMENT AND ADVICE

The Canadian Information Centre for International Credentials, 252 Bloor West, Suite 5–200, Toronto, ON M5S 1V5. Tel: (416) 964 2551. Fax: (416) 964 2296. Document Evaluation Service, York University, 4700 Keele St, North York, ON M3J 1P3. Tel: (416) 736 5217. Fax: (416) 736 5898. International Credential Assessment Service of Canada, Inc. **British Columbia**: 528 Carnarvon St, New Westminster, BC V3L 1C4. **Ontario**: 111 Bond St, Toronto, ON M5B 1Y2. Tel: (519) 763 7272. Fax: (416) 269 7612. **Nova Scotia**: PO Box 266, Wolfville, NS B0P IX0. ICES, Opening Learning Agency, 4355 Mathissi Pl, Burnaby, BC V5G 4S8. Tel: (604) 431 3054. Fax: (604) 431 3382. International Qualifications Assessment Service, Alberta Labour, Professions and Occupations, 5th Floor, Peace Hills Trust Tower, 10011-109 St, Edmonton, AB T5J 3S8. Tel: (403) 427 2655. Fax: (403) 422 9734.

### For the Province of Québec only

Service des équivalences, Ministère des Affaires internationales, de l'Immigration et des Communautés culturelles, Direction des équivalences et de l'administration des ententes de sécurité sociale, 360 rue McGill, Montréal, Québec H2Y 2E9. Tel: (514) 873 5647. Fax: (514) 873 8701.

## ECONOMIC DEVELOPMENT DEPARTMENTS – PROVINCIAL

**Alberta**. Alberta Economic Development and Trade, Policy Development and Coordination, 9th Floor, Sterling Place, 9940 106 Street, Edmonton, AB T5K 2P6. Tel: (403) 427 3627. Fax: (403) 427 5922.
**British Columbia**. Ministry of Economic Development, Small Business and Trade, 712 Yates Street, Victoria, BC V8V 1X4. Tel: (604) 387 0275. Fax: (604) 387 8035.
**Manitoba**. Manitoba Industry, Trade and Tourism, 6th Floor, 155 Carlton Street, Winnipeg, MB R3C 3H8. Tel: (204) 945 2024. Fax: (204) 945 1354.
**New Brunswick**. Department of Economic Development and Tourism,

Planning and Agreements Division, PO Box 6000, Fredericton, NB E3B 5H1. Tel: (506) 453 2629. Fax: (506) 453 7904.

**Newfoundland.** Economic Research and Analysis Division, Cabinet Secretariat, Department of Executive Council, Confederation Building, PO Box 8700, St John's, NF A1B 4J6. Tel: (709) 729 3256. Fax: (709) 729 6944.

**Newfoundland.** Department of Industry, Trade and Technology, Economic and Trade Analysis Division, PO Box 8700, St John's, NF A1B 4J6. Tel: (709) 729 2796. Fax: (709) 729 5936.

**Nova Scotia.** Department of Economic Development, PO Box 519, Halifax, NS B3J 2R7. Tel: (902) 424 8920. Fax: (902) 424 5739.

**Ontario.** Office of Economic Policy, Ministry of Treasury and Economics, 5th Floor, Frost Building, N Toronto, ON M7A 1Y7. Tel: (416) 325 0850. Fax: (416) 325 0841.

**Prince Edward Island.** Economics, Statistics and Fiscal Analysis Division, Department of Finance, PO Box 2000, Charlottetown, PE C1A 7N8. Tel: (902) 368 4030. Fax: (902) 368 5544.

**Québec.** Ministère de la Main-d'oeuvre, de la Sécurité du revenu et de la Formation professionnelle Communications, 255 boul. Cremazie Est, Montréal, PQ H2M 1L5. Tel: (514) 873 2145. Fax:( 514) 873 0280.

Office de Planification et développement du Québec Service des Communications, Complexe G, Aile St-Amable, 1060 rue Conroy, Québec, PQ G1R 5E6. Tel: (418) 643 3285. Fax: (418) 643 4719.

**Saskatchewan.** Department of Finance, Economic and Fiscal Policy Branch, 6th Floor, 2350 Albert Street, Regina, SK S4P 4A6. Tel: (306) 787 6724. Fax: (306) 787 1426.

Policy and Coordination Branch, Saskatchewan Economic Development, 1919 Saskatchewan Drive, Regina, SK S4P 1C8. Tel: (306) 787 1672. Fax: (306) 787 2198.

**Northwest Territories.** Policy and Planning Department of Economic Development and Tourism, PO Box 1320, Yellowknife, NT X1A 2L9. Tel: (403) 873 7318. Fax: (403) 873 0101.

**Yukon.** Department of Economic Development, PO Box 2703, Whitehorse, YT Y1A 2C6. Tel: (403) 667 5466. Fax: (403) 667 3205.

**Montreal (Region).** Economic Development Office, Montreal Urban Community, 770 Sherbrooke Street, W #1210, Montreal, PQ H3A 1G1. Tel: (514) 280 4242. Fax: (514) 280 4266.

**Toronto.** Planning and Development Dept, Economic Development Division, 2nd Floor, East Tower City Hall, Toronto, ON M5H 2N2. Tel: (416) 392 7571. Fax: (416) 392 0675.

## IMMIGRATION ATTORNEYS

Brownstein, Brownstein & Associates, 1310 Greene Avenue, Suite 750, Montreal, PQ H3Z 2B2. Tel: (514) 939 9559. Fax: (514) 939 2289.

Codina Partners International, Suite 708, 390 Bay Street, Toronto, ON M5H

2Y2. Tel: (416) 361 1404. Fax: (416) 361 1390.
Green & Spiegel, Standard Life Centre, 121 King Street West, Suite 2200, Toronto, ON M5H 3T9. Tel: (416) 862 7880. Fax: (416) 862 1698.
John Paul Evans, 962 The East Mall, Etobicoke, ON M9B 6K1. Tel: (416) 620 7300. Fax: (416) 620 1679.
Karas & Associates, 38 Queen Anne Street, London W1M 9LB. Tel: (0171) 637 8865. Fax: (0171) 637 2630.
Mamann Kranc, 212 King Street, Suite 410, Toronto, ON M5H 1K5. Tel: (416) 599 3000. Fax: (416) 599 5582.
Stewart Roper & Associates, 95 Wellington Street West, Suite 906, PO Box 40, Toronto, ON M5J 2N7. Tel: (416) 368 7881. Fax: (416) 368 0549.
Tkatch & Young, 22 College Street, Suite 488, Toronto, ON M5G 1K2. Tel: (416) 968 033376. Fax: (416) 968 0232.

## IMMIGRATION CONSULTANTS

Ambler Collins, Eden House, 59 Fulham High Street, London SW6 3JJ. Tel: (0171) 371 0213. Fax: (0171) 736 8841.
Buysse Immigration Consultancy, 3019 Harvester Road, Burlington, ON L7N 3G4. Tel: (905) 333 1913. Fax: (905) 333 5958.
Commonwealth Jobsearch, Oxford House, College Court, Commercial Road, Swindon, Wilts SN1 1PZ. Tel: (01793) 535300. Fax: (01793) 542554.
Robert P Downe, 424 Hensall Circle, Suite 102, Missassauga, ON L5A 1X7. Tel: (905) 566 0585. Fax: (905) 848 9863.
Emigration Consultancy Services, De Salis Court, Hampton Lovett, Droitwich, Worcs WR9 0NX. Tel: (01905) 795949.
Hall & Associates, 500 Chesham House, 150 Regent Street, London W1R 5FA. Tel: (0171) 439 6288. Fax: (0171) 734 4166.
IAS, PO Box 3003, Rockville, Maryland 20847, USA. Fax: (301) 770 9549.
Katz Consulting, 38 Queen Anne Street, London W1M 9LB. Tel: (0171) 637 8865. Fax: (0171) 637 2630.
M&M Consultants (Canada) Ltd, Canada House Business Centre, 272 Field End Road, Eastcote HA4 9NA. Tel: (0181) 429 3102. Fax: (0181) 866 4170.
R A Melnyk Immigration Services Inc, 1 Yonge Street, Suite 1801, Toronto, ON M5E 1W7. Tel: (905) 715 7360. Fax: (905) 715 7361.
Skiba & Associates, 23 High Street, Moncton, NB E1C 6B4. Tel: (506) 756 2723. Fax: (506) 383 8998.
Sparling, Billings & Kei Inc, Suite 211, 6 Lansing Square, Toronto, ON M2J 1T5. Tel: (416) 495 7965. Fax: (416) 495 1849.
Thornton & Company, 82 Galpins Road, Thornton Heath, Surrey CR7 6ED. Tel: (0181) 684 5916.

## NEWSPAPERS (DAILY) PUBLISHED IN CANADA'S MAJOR CITIES

### Alberta

**Calgary.** *Calgary Herald*, Southam Inc, 215 16 Street SE, (PO Box 2400), Stn M T2P 0W8.

*The Calgary Sun*, 2615 12 Street NE T2E 7W9.

**Edmonton.** *The Edmonton Journal*, Southam Inc, PO Box 2421, T5J 2S6.

*The Edmonton Sun*, #250, 4990 92 Avenue, T6B 3A1.

### British Columbia

**Vancouver.** *The Vancouver Sun*, Pacific Press Ltd, 2250 Granville Street, V6H 3G2.

*The Province*, Pacific Press Ltd, 2250 Granville Street, V6H 3G2.

**Victoria.** *Times Colonist*, Canadian Newspapers Co Ltd, 2621 Douglas Street, V8T 4M2.

### Manitoba

**Winnipeg.** *Winnipeg Free Press*, Canadian Newspapers Co Ltd, 1355 Mountain Avenue, R2X 3B6.

*The Winnipeg Sun*, 1700 Church Avenue, R2X 3A2.

### New Brunswick

**Fredericton.** *Daily Gleaner*, PO Box 3370, E3B 5A2.

**Saint John.** *The Telegraph-Journal*, Crown Street at Union, (PO Box 2350), E2L 3V8.

*The Evening Times-Globe*, Crown Street at Union, (PO Box 2350), E2L 3V8.

### Newfoundland

**St John's.** *The Evening Telegram*, Columbus Drive, (PO Box 5970), A1C 5X7.

### Nova Scotia

**Halifax.** *The Chronicle-Herald*, 1650 Argyle Street, B3J 2T2.

*The Mail-Star*, 1650 Argyle Street, B3J 2T2.

*The Daily News*, 202 Brownlow Avenue, Dartmouth, (PO Box 8330), Stn A, B3K 5N1.

**Sydney.** *Cape Breton Post*, 255 George Street, B1P 6K6.

### Ontario

**Kingston.** *Whig-Standard*, 306 King Street E, K7L 4Z7.

**Kitchener.** *Kitchener-Waterloo Record*, 255 Fairway Road S, N2G 4E5.

**Ottawa.** *Le Droit*, 47 Clarence Street, #222 (PO Box 8660) Stn T, K1G 3J9.

*The Ottawa Citizen*, Southam Inc, 1101 Baxter Road, (PO Box 5020), K2C 3M4.

*Ottawa Sun*, 380 Hunt Club Road, (PO Box 9729), Stn T, K1G 5H7.
**Toronto.** *The Financial Post*, 333 King Street E, M5A 4N2.
*The Globe and Mail*, 444 Front Street W, M5V 2S9.
*The Toronto Star*, One Yonge Street, M5E 1E6.
*The Toronto Sun*, 333 King Street E, M5A 3X5.

### Prince Edward Island
**Charlottetown.** *Guardian*, 165 Prince Street, C1A 4R7.
*Patriot*, 165 Prince Street, C1A 4R7.

### Québec
**Montréal.** *Le Devoir*, 211 rue St-Sacrement, H2Y 1X1.
*The Gazette*, 250 St-Antoine Ouest, H2Y 3R7.
*Le Journal de Montréal*, Groupe Québécor Inc, 4545 Frontenac, H2H 2R7.
*La Presse*, 7 St-Jacques, H2Y 1K9.
**Québec.** *Le Journal de Québec*, Groupe Québécor Inc, 450 rue Béchard, Ville de
    Vanier, G1M 2E9.
*Le Soleil*, 390 St-Vallier Est, G1K 7J6.

### Saskatchewan
**Regina.** *The Leader-Post*, 1964 Park Street, S4P 3G4.
**Saskatoon.** *Star-Phoenix*, Armdale Publishers Ltd, 204 5th Avenue N, S7K
    2P1.

### Yukon and Northwest Territories
**Whitehorse.** *The Whitehorse Star*, 2149 2nd Avenue, YT, Y1A 1C5.
**Yellowknife.** *L'Aquilon* (Fri), PO Box 1325, NWT, X1A 2N9.
*The Press Independent* (Fri), 5120 49 Street, NWT, X1A 1P8.
*News/North* (Mon), PO Box 2820, NWT, X1A 2R1.
*Yellowknifer* (Wed), PO Box 2820, NWT, X1A 2R1.

## OCCUPATIONAL TRAINING – PROVINCIAL DEPARTMENTS

**Alberta.** Career Information Hotline, Alberta Career Development and
    Employment, 9th Floor, CityCentre Building, 10155 102 Street, Edmon-
    ton, AB T5J 4L5. Tel: (403) 422 4266. Fax: (403) 422 0408.
**British Columbia.** Skills Development Division, Ministry of Advanced
    Education, Training and Technology, 1st Floor, 838 Fort Street, Victoria,
    BC V8V 1X4. Tel: (604) 387 3698. Fax: (604) 356 0008.
**Manitoba.** Manitoba Education and Training, Post-Secondary, Adult and
    Continuing Education Division, 4th Floor, 185 Carlton Street, Winnipeg,
    MB R3C 3J1. Tel: (204) 945 4304. Fax: (204) 945 1792.
**New Brunswick.** Department of Advanced Education and Labour, (416 York
    Street), PO Box 6000, Fredericton, NB E3B 5H1. Tel: (506) 453 2597. Fax:
    (506) 453 7913.

**Newfoundland.** Division of Post-Secondary Education, Department of Education, PO Box 8700, St John's, NF A1B 4J6. Tel: (709) 729 4324. Fax: (709) 729 5896.

**Nova Scotia.** Community College Branch, Department of Education, PO Box 578, Halifax, NS B3J 2S9. Tel: (902) 424 4060. Fax: (902) 424 0519.

**Ontario.** Ministry of Skills Development, Skills Development Division, 101 Bloor Street West, 12th Floor, Toronto, ON M5S 1P7. Tel: (416) 967 8444. Fax: (416) 965 7144.

**Prince Edward Island.** Apprentice Branch, Department of Industry, PO Box 2000, Charlottetown, PE C1A 7NB. Tel: (902) 368 4460. Fax: (902) 368 4224.

**Quebec.** (Colleges Cegep) Ministère de l'Enseignement Supérieur, et de la Science, Direction des Communications, 1033 rue De La Chevrotière, Edifice Marie-Guyart, 19e étage, Québec, PQ G1R 5K9. Tel: (418) 643 6788. Fax: (418) 643 8651.

**Saskatchewan.** Training Plans and College Liaison Branch, Saskatchewan Education, 2220 College Avenue, Regina, SK S4P 3V7. Tel: (306) 787 5594. Fax: (306) 787 5594.

## PET TRAVEL SPECIALISTS

Airpets Oceanic, Willowslea Farm Kennels, Spout Lane North, Stanwell Moor, Staines, Middx TW19 6BW. Tel: (01753) 685571. Fax: (01753) 681655.

Golden Arrow Shippers, Lydbury North, Shropshire SY7 8AY. Tel: (01588) 240/606. Fax: (01588) 414.

Transpet, 160 Chingford Mount Road, London E4 9BS. Tel: (0181) 529 0979/ 0112. Fax: (0181) 529 2563.

Worldwide Animal Travel, 43 London Road, Brentwood, Essex CM14 4NN. Tel: (01277) 231611. Fax: (0181) 552 5592.

## PLACEMENT AGENCIES

### Recruiting internationally

Beechwood Recruitment Ltd, 221 High Street, London W3 9BY.

CC & CP International Ltd, 26–28 Bedford Row, London WC1R 4HF. Tel: (0171) 242 8998.

William Channing, Clarendon House, 11–12 Clifford St, London W1X 1RB. Tel: (0171) 491 1338.

Commonwealth Placements, Oxford House, College Court, Commercial Road, Swindon, Wilts SN1 1PZ. Tel: (01793) 612222. Fax: (01793) 542554.

Consultancy International Ltd, 40–41 Pall Mall, London SW1Y 5JG.

Dare Personnel Inc, 275 Slater Street, Suite 900, Ottawa, ON K1P 5H9. Tel: (613) 238 4485. Fax: (613) 238 3754. Internet: Dare@hypernet.on.ca.

Drake Executive, Drake International, London. Tel: (0171) 245 1040.

Executive Recruitment Services, Boundary Way, Hemel Hempstead, Herts HP2 7RX. Tel: (01442) 231691. Fax: (01442) 230063.
Grove Personnel Ltd, 46–48 Southbourne Grove, Bournemouth BH6 3RB. Tel: (01202) 417533. Fax: (01202) 421746.
Inter Engineering Consultancy Ltd, 22–24 Buckingham Palace Road, London SW1W 0QP.
International Hospitals Group (IBG), Stoke Park, Stoke Poges, Berks SL2 4HS.
International Secretaries, 174 New Bond Street, London W1Y 9PT.
JvB Consultancy, 10 Station Road, Blackwell, Worcs. Tel: (0121) 445 5344.
Offshore Specialist Appointments, Tower Hill Steps, 16 Le Brodage, St Peter Port, Guernsey.
The Oz Link, 3 New St, Chulmleigh, Devon EX18 7DB. Tel: (01769) 581318 (mobile 0374 159350).
Target Data Services Inc, 2396–2398 Dunwin Drive, Mississauga, ON L5L 1J9. Tel: (905) 858 7810. Fax: (905) 858 0112.
TRC Ltd, Walmar House, 296 Regent Street, London W1R 5HD.

## Temporary/holiday work: information and assistance

BUNAC (British Universities North American Club), 16 Bowling Green Lane, London EC1R 0BD. Tel: (0171) 251 3472.
Christian Movement for Peace, Bethnal Green United Reform Church, Pott Street, London E2 0EF. Tel: (0171) 729 1877.
Frontiers Foundation/Operation Beaver, 2615 Danforth Avenue, Suite 203, Toronto, ON.
GAP Activity Projects Ltd, Gap House, 44 Queens Road, Reading, Berks RG1 4BB. Tel: (01734) 594914.
United Nations Association International Youth Service, Temple of Peace, Cathay's Park, Cardiff CF1 3AP. Tel: (01222) 223088.

## Specialising in nannies, au pairs and mothers' helps

Anglia Au Pair Agency, 70 Southsea Avenue, Leigh-on-Sea, Essex SS9 2BJ. Tel: (01702) 471648.
Avalon Agency, 30 Queen's Road, Brighton, East Sussex BN1 3XA. Tel: (01273) 26866.
Euro Employment Centre, 42 Upper Union Arcade, Bury, Lancs BL9 0QF. Tel: (0161) 797 6400.
Janet White Employment Agency, 67 Jackson Avenue, Leeds LS8 1NS. Tel: (01532) 666507.
Jolaine Agency, 18 Escot Way, Barnet, Herts EN5 3AN.
Nash Personnel Services, Homelands House, Bines Road, Partridge Green, Horsham, Sussex RH13 8EQ. Tel: (01403) 711436.
Solihull Au Pair and Nanny Agency, 1565 Stratford Road, Hall Green, Birmingham B28 9JA. Tel: (0121) 733 6444. Fax: (0121) 733 6555.
Universal Care, 1 Chester House, 9 Windsor End, Beaconsfield, Bucks HP9

2JJ. Tel: (01494) 678811.

## PROFESSIONAL ASSOCIATIONS – CANADA

**Accounting.** Canadian Association of Certified Executive Accountants, PO Box 43038, Ottawa, ON K1J 9M4. Tel: (613) 745 5672. Fax: (613) 745 6754. Canadian Institute of Chartered Accountants, 277 Wellington Street West, Toronto, ON M5V 3H2. Tel: (416) 977 3222. Fax: (416) 977 8585. Canadian Institute of Financial Accountants, PO Box 43028, Ottawa, ON K1J 9M4. Tel: (613) 745 3441.

**Advertising and marketing.** Business/Professional Advertising Association, 3rd Floor, 317 Place d'Youville, Montréal, PQ H2Y 2B5. Canadian Institute of Marketing, 41 Capital Drive, Nepean, ON K2G 0E7. Tel: (613) 727 0954. Fax: (613) 228 8398.

**Agriculture and farming.** Agricultural Institute of Canada, #907, 151 Slater Street, Ottawa, ON K1P 5H4. Tel: (613) 232 9459. Fax: (613) 594 5190. Canadian Federation of Agriculture, #1101, 75 Albert Street, Ottawa, ON K1P 5E7. Tel: (613) 236 9997. Fax: (613) 236 5749.

**Animal breeding.** Canadian Cattlemen's Association, #215, 6715-8 Street Northeast, Calgary, AB T2E 7H7. Tel: (403) 275 9242. Fax: (403) 374 0007.

**Animals and animal science.** Canadian Veterinary Medical Association, 339 Booth Street, Ottawa, ON K1R 7K1. Tel: (613) 236 1162. Fax: (613) 236 9681.

**Apparel, textiles, fashion and footwear.** Canadian Allied Textile Trades Association, 49 Front Street East, Toronto, ON M5E 1B3. Tel: (416) 363 4266.

**Architecture.** Royal Architectural Institute of Canada, #330, 55 Murray Street, Ottawa, ON K1N 5M3. Tel: (613) 232 7165. Fax: (613) 232 7559.

**Arts.** Council for Business and the Arts in Canada, 401 Bay Street, Box 7, Toronto, ON M5H 2Y4. Tel: (416) 869 3016.

**Automotive.** Association of International Automobile Manufacturers of Canada, #700, 210 Dundas Street West, Toronto, ON M5G 2EB. Tel: (416) 595 5333. Fax: (416) 595 8226. National Automotive Trades Association of Canada, 2175 Royal Windsor Drive, Mississauga, ON L5J 1K5. Tel: (416) 855 1590.

**Aviation and aerospace.** Aerospace Industries Association of Canada, #1200, 60 Queen Street, Ottawa, ON K1P 5Y7. Tel: (613) 232 4297. Fax: (613) 232 1142.

**Broadcasting.** Canadian Association of Broadcasters, PO Box 627, Station B, Ottawa, ON K1P 5S2. Tel: (613) 233 4035. Fax: (613) 233 6961.

**Building and construction.** Canadian Construction Association, 85 Albert Street, 10th Floor, Ottawa, ON K1P 6A4. Tel: (613) 236 9455. Fax: (613) 236 9526.

**Business.** Canadian Council of Better Business Bureaux, #219, 2180 Steeles Avenue West, Concord, ON L4K 2Z5. Tel: (416) 669 1248. Fax: (416) 669

4786.

**Chemical industry.** Canadian Chemical Producers' Association, #805, 350 Sparks Street, Ottawa, ON K1R 7S8. Tel: (613) 237 6215. Fax: (613) 237 4061.

**Consumers.** Canadian Society of Consumer Affairs Professionals in Business, PO Box 335, Station Q, Toronto, ON M4T 2M5.

**Dental.** Canadian Dental Association, 1815 Alta Vista Drive, Ottawa, ON K1G 3Y6. Tel: (613) 523 1770. Fax: (613) 523 7736.

**Economics.** Canadian Economics Association, Stephen Leacock Building, Department of Economics, McGill University, 855 Sherbrooke Street West, Montreal, PQ H3A 2T7. Tel: (514) 398 4830.

**Education.** Association of Universities and Colleges of Canada, 151 Slater Street, Ottawa, ON K1P 5N1. Tel: (613) 563 1236. Fax: (613) 563 9745. Canadian Education Association, #8-200, 252 Bloor Street West, Toronto, ON M5V 1V5. Tel: (416) 924 7721. Fax: (416) 924 3188.

**Energy.** Canadian Institute of Energy, #229-640 5 Avenue Southwest, Calgary, AB T2P 0M6. Tel: (403) 262 6969.

**Engineering and technology.** Canadian Council of Professional Engineers, #401, 116 Albert Street, Ottawa, ON K1P 5G3. Tel: (613) 232 2474. Fax: (613) 230 5759.

**Equipment and machinery.** Machinery and Equipment Manufacturers' Association of Canada, #701, 116 Albert Street, Ottawa, ON K1P 5G3. Tel: (613) 232 7213.

**Film and video.** Canadian Film & Television Production Association, #404, 663 Yonge Street, Toronto, ON M4Y 2A4. Tel: (416) 927 8942. Fax: (416) 922 4038.

**Finance.** Canadian Institute of Credit & Financial Management, #501, 5090 Explorer Drive, Mississauga, ON L4W 3T9. Tel: (416) 629 9805. Fax: (416) 629 9809.

**Fisheries and fishing industry.** Fisheries Council of Canada, #806, 141 Laurier Avenue West, Ottawa, ON K1P 5J3. Tel: (613) 238 7751. Fax: (613) 238 3542.

**Food and beverage industry.** Canadian Dairy & Food Industries Supply Association, 1148 Vanier Drive, Mississauga, ON L5H 3X1. Tel: (416) 278 6496.

**Forestry and forest products.** Canadian Forestry Association, #203, 185 Somerset Street West, Ottawa, ON K2P 0J2. Tel: (613) 232 1815. Fax: (613) 232 4210.

**Gas and oil.** Petroleum Services Association of Canada, #1202, 500 – 4 Avenue SW, Calgary, AB T2P 0M2. Tel: (403) 264 4195. Fax: (403) 263 3796.

**Health and medical.** The Canadian Medical Association, 1867 Alta Vista Drive, PO Box 8650, Ottawa, ON K1G 3Y6. Tel: (613) 731 9331. Fax: (613) 731 9013.

**Hospitals.** Canadian Hospital Association, #100, 17 York Street, Ottawa, ON K1N 9J6. Tel: (613) 238 8005.

**Industrial development.** Canadian Advanced Technology Association, #388

Albert Street, 2nd Floor, Ottawa, ON K1P 5H9. Tel: (613) 236 6550. Fax: (613) 236 8189.

**Information management.** Association of Information Systems Professionals – Canadian Region, Saskatchewan Health, #203, 4902 Queen Street, Regina, SK S4S 6X4. Tel: (306) 787 3110.

**Insurance industry.** Association of Canadian Insurers, #2000, 390 Bay Street, Toronto, ON M5H 2Y2. Tel: (416) 362 5286.
Insurance Brokers Association of Canada, #801, 141 Adelaide Street West, Toronto, ON M5H 3L5. Tel: (416) 367 1831. Fax: (416) 367 3687.

**Language, linguistics.** Canadian Translators & Interpreters Council, #1402, 1 rue Nicholas, Ottawa, ON K1N 7B7. Tel: (613) 233 6395. Fax: (613) 233 7473.

**Law.** Canadian Bar Association, #902, 50 O'Connor Street, Ottawa, ON K1P 6L2. Tel: (613) 237 2925. Fax: (613) 237 0185.

**Management and administration.** Institute of Chartered Secretaries & Administrators in Canada, #301, 250 Consumers Road, Willowdale, ON M2J 4Y6. Tel: (416) 494 3757. Fax: (416) 495 8723.
Professional Secretaries International, 10502 NW Ambassador Drive, PO Box 20404, Kansas City, MO 64195-0404 USA. Tel: (816) 891 6600.

**Manufacturing.** Canadian Manufacturers' Association, #1400, One Yonge Street, Toronto, ON M5E 1J9. Tel: (416) 363 7261. Fax: (416) 363 3779.

**Mines and mineral products.** Canadian Institute of Mining, Metallurgy & Petroleum, Xerox Tower, #1210, 3400 Masionneuve Blvd West, Montréal, PQ H3Z 3B8. Tel: (514) 939 2710. Fax: (514) 939 2714.

**Music.** Canadian Academy of Recording Arts & Sciences, 124 Merton Street, 3rd Floor, Toronto, ON M4S 2Z2. Tel: (416) 485 3135. Fax: (416) 485 4978.

**Nursing.** Canadian Nurses Association, 50 The Driveway, Ottawa, ON K2P 1E2. Tel: (613) 237 2133. Fax: (613) 237 3520.

**Pharmaceutical.** Canadian Pharmaceutical Association, 1785 Alta Vista Drive, 2nd Floor, Ottawa, ON K1G 3Y6. Tel: (613) 523 7877 Fax: (613) 523 0445.

**Printing industry and graphic arts.** Canadian Printing Industries Association, #906, 75 Albert Street, Ottawa, ON K1P 5E7. Tel: (613) 236 7208. Fax: (613) 236 8169.

**Public relations.** Canadian Public Relations Society, #720, 220 Laurier Avenue West, Ottawa, ON K1P 5Z9. Tel: (613) 232 1222. Fax: (613) 232 0565.

**Publishing.** Association of Canadian Publishers, 260 King Street East, Toronto, ON M5A 1K3. Tel: (416) 361 1408. Fax: (416) 361 0643.

**Real estate.** The Canadian Real Estate Association, Place de Ville, Tower A #2100, 320 Queen Street, Ottawa, ON K1R 5A3. Tel: (613) 234 3372. Fax: (613) 234 2567.

**Restaurants, bars, food services.** Canadian Restaurant & Foodservices Association, #1202, 80 Bloor Street West, Toronto, ON M5S 2V1. Tel: (416) 923 8416. Fax: (418) 923 1450.

**Retail trade.** Retail Merchants Association of Canada Inc, 1780 Birchmount Road, Scarborough, ON M1P 2H8. Tel: (416) 291 7903. Fax: (416) 291 5635.

**Standards and testing**. Canadian Association of Quality Assurance Professionals, #409, 1 Eva Road, Etobicoke, ON M9C 4Z5. Tel: (416) 626 0102.
**Steel and metal industries**. Canadian Steel Trade & Employment Congress, #803, 234 Eglinton Avenue East, Toronto, ON M4P 1K7. Tel: (416) 480 1797. Fax: (416) 480 2986.
**Tourism and travel**. Tourism Industry Association of Canada, #1016, 130 Albert Street, Ottawa, ON K1P 5G4. Tel: (613) 238 3883. Fax: (613) 238 3878.
**Transportation**. Canadian Institute of Traffic & Transportation, 145 Berkeley Street, 5th Floor, Toronto, ON M5A 2X1. Tel: (416) 363 5696. Fax: (416) 363 5698.

## REMOVAL FIRMS – INTERNATIONAL

Abels, branches throughout the UK. Tel: (freephone) 0800 626769.
Anglo Canadian Connections Ltd, 18 Springfield Road, Linlithgow, West Lothian EH49 7JJ.
Anglo Pacific International Plc, Unit 1, Bush Industrial Estate, Standard Road, North Acton, London NW10 6DF. Tel: (0181) 965 1234. Fax: (0181) 965 4954.
Bishop's, Blatchpack, Kestrel Way, Sowton Industrial Estate, Exeter EX2 7PA. Tel: (01392) 420404. Fax: (01392) 423851.
Brewer & Turnbull, Harrow, Middx HA1 1AD. Tel: (freephone) 0500 749126.
Copsey, Danes Road, Romford, Essex RM7 0HL. Tel: (freephone) 0800 289 658.
Davies Turner Worldwide Movers, Overseas House, Stewarts Road, London SW8 4UG. Tel: (0171) 622 4393.
Double Overseas Removals Ltd, Movements House, Ajax Works, Hertford Road, Barking, Essex IG11 8BW. Tel: (0181) 591 6929. Fax: (0181) 594 5935.
Econopak Removals Ltd, Unit K, Abbey Wharf Industrial Estate, Kingsbridge Road, Barking, Essex IG11 0BT. Tel: (0181) 591 3434.
Interpack Worldwide Ltd, Unit 11, Hanover West Trading Estate, 161 Acton Lane, London NW10. Tel: (0181) 965 5550. Fax: (0181) 453 0544.
John Mason International, Freepost, Liverpool L36 6AE.
Personal Shipping Services, 8 Redcross Way, London Bridge, London SE1 9HR. Tel: (0171) 407 6606.
Pickfords, 492 Great Cambridge Road, Enfield, Middx EN1 3SA. Tel: (0181) 367 0045 or (freephone) 0800 289 229.
Robinsons International Removers, Freepost, 24 Somerton Road, London NW2 3YP. Tel: (0181) 452 5441.
Scotpac, Kilsyth Road, Kirkintilloch, Scotland. Tel: (0141) 776 7191/5194. .Fax: (0141) 777 6138.
White & Company Canadian Moving Services, Hillsons Road, Botley, Southampton SO3 2DY. Tel: (01489) 783343.

## TOURIST BOARDS – PROVINCIAL

Provincial Government of Alberta, 1 Mount Street, London W1Y 5AA.

Provincial Government of British Columbia, British Columbia House, 1 Regent Street, London SW1Y 4NS.

Travel Manitoba, 7th Floor, 155 Carlton St, Winnipeg, Manitoba, Canada R3C 3H8.

Government of New Brunswick, Glockengiesserwall 17, D-20095 Hamburg, Germany.

Newfoundland and Labrador Dept of Tourism, PO Box 8730, St John's, Newfoundland, Canada A1B 4J6.

Northwest Territories Dept of Tourism, Yellowknife, Northwest Territories, Canada X1A 2L9.

Provincial Government of Nova Scotia, Crusade House, 14 Pall Mall, London SW1X 7LY.

Provincial Government of Ontario, 21 Knightsbridge, London SW1X 7LY.

Prince Edward Island Dept of Tourism, PO Box 940, Charlottetown, PEI, Canada C1A 7M5.

Provincial Government of Quebec, 59 Pall Mall, London SW1Y 5JH.

Tourism Saskatchewan, 1919 Saskatchewan Drive, Regina, Saskatchewan, Canada S4P 3V7.

Tourism Yukon, PO Box 2703, Whitehorse, Yukon, Canada Y1A 2C6.

## TRADES UNIONS – GENERAL

Most of the individual trades unions will be affiliated with one of the following.

Canadian Federation of Labour, 107 Sparks Street, Suite 300, Ottawa, ON K1P 5B5. Tel: (613) 234 4141. Fax: (613) 234 5188.

Canadian Labour Congress, 284 Riverside Drive, Ottawa, ON K1V 8X7. Tel: (613) 521 3400. Fax: (613) 521 4655.

Centrale de l'enseignement du Québec, 9405 rue Sherbrooke est, Montréal, PQ H1L 6B3. Tel: (514) 356 8888. Fax: (514) 356 9999.

Confederation of Canadian Unions, 1331½<sup>A</sup> St Clair Avenue West, Toronto, ON M6E 1C3. Tel: (416) 651 5627. Fax: (416) 598 2089.

Confédération des syndicats nationaux, 1601 ave de Lorimier, Montréal, PQ H2K 4M5. Tel: (514) 598 2121. Fax: (514) 598 2089.

## OTHER USEFUL ADDRESSES

The Association of Professional Placement Agencies and Consultants, 114 Richmond St East, Suite L-109, Toronto ON M5C 1P1. Tel: (416) 362 0983. Fax: (416) 360 5478.

Barkers Worldwide Publications, 155 Mayberry Rd, Woking, Surrey GU21 7JR. Tel: (01483) 776141. Fax: (01483) 776141.

Canadian Bureau for International Education, 85 Albert St, 14th Flr, Ottawa, ON K1P 6A4.

Canada Information Services, Suite 421, 253 College St, Toronto, ON M5T 1R5.

The Canadian Society for the Study of Higher Education, #1001, 151 Slater Street, Ottawa, ON K1P 5N1.

The Centre for International Briefing, Farnham Castle, Surrey GU9 0AG. Tel: (01252) 721194. Fax: (01252) 711283.

City of London Business Library, 1 Brewers Hall Garden, London Wall, London EC2V 5BY. Tel: (0171) 638 8215.

Comparative Education Service, Room 202, 214 College St, Toronto, ON M5T 2Z9. Tel: (416) 978 2185. Fax: (416) 978 7022.

The Conference of Independent Schools, PO Box 182, Port Hope, ON L1A 3W3.

Department of Social Security, Overseas Branch, Newcastle upon Tyne NE98 1YX. Tel: (0191) 225 7341.

Employment & Immigration Canada, Public Inquiries Centre, Public Affairs Branch, 140 Promenade du Portage, Phase IV, Hull, PQ K1A 0J9. Tel: (819) 994 6313. Fax: (819) 994 0116.

Expat Network, International House, 500 Purley Way, Croydon, Surrey CR9 4NZ.

The Federation of Temporary Help Services, 409, 1 Eva Road, Etobicoke, ON M9C 4Z5.

The Immigration and Medical Division of the Canadian High Commission, 38 Grosvenor St, London W1X 0AA. Tel: (0171) 629 9492. Fax: (0171) 491 3968.

The League for the Exchange of Commonwealth Teachers, Commonwealth House, 7 Lion Yard, Tremadoc Road, Clapham, London SW4 7NQ. Tel: (0171) 498 1101. Fax: (0171) 720 5403.

The Ministry of Agriculture, Hook Rise South, Tolworth, Surbiton, Surrey KT7 6NF. Tel: (0181) 330 8183.

Moving Publications Ltd, 44 Upjohn St, Ste 100, Don Mills, ON M3B 2W1. Tel: (416) 441 1168. Fax: (416) 441 1641.

PA Personal Services, Hyde Park House, 60a Knightsbridge, London SW1 7LE.

Public Service Commission, Training Programs Branch, Ottawa, ON K1A 0M7. Tel: (613) 991 4636. Fax: (613) 999 7859.

Service d'Immigration du Québec, Délégation générale du Québec, 46 avenue des Arts, 7 étage, 1040 Bruxelles, Belgium. Tel: (322) 512 0036. Fax: (332) 514 2641.

Society for Educational Visits & Exchanges in Canada, 57 Auriga Dr, Nepean, ON K2E 8B2. Tel: (613) 998 3760. Fax: (613) 998 7094.

Youth and Student Information Association of Student Councils, 171 College St, Toronto, ON M5T 1PZ.

# Index